The New Protreptic
– The Concept and the Art

Ole Fogh Kirkeby

The New Protreptic
– The Concept and the Art

The New Protreptic – The Concept and the Art
© Copenhagen Business School Press, 2009
Printed in Denmark by Narayana Press, Gylling
Typeset: Narayana Press
Cover design by Klahr | Graphic Design
1st edition 2009

ISBN 978-87-630-0233-2

Distribution:

Scandinavia
DBK, Mimersvej 4
DK-4600 Køge, Denmark
Tel +45 3269 7788
Fax +45 3269 7789

North America
International Specialized Book Services
920 NE 58th Street, Suite 300
Portland, OR 97213-3786
Tel +1 800 944 6190
Fax +1 503 280 8832
Email: orders@isbs.com

Rest of the World
Marston Book Services, P.O. Box 269
Abingdon, Oxfordshire, OX14 4YN, UK
Tel +44 (0) 1235 465500
Fax +44 (0) 1235 465655
Email: client.orders@marston.co.uk

Contents

Acknowledgements

I am utterly indebted to my friend professor Daved Barry for thoroughly and patiently revising the text, transforming it both into acceptable English, and contributing considerably with ameliorations in relation to its meta-language and to its content. To him I cannot be grateful enough. I am also deeply grateful to Matthew Hancocks to have undertaken the laborious task to read the manuscript twice having improved it considerably.

I should also like to thank my friends and colleagues who joined me on the journey into the beautiful foreign country of protreptic, both in theory and practice, among them partners from Copenhagen Coaching Centre, Andreas Bering, Jens Jensen, and Mette Mejlhede, and my friend Ph.D.-student Tobias Dam Hede. Two years ago, I wrote a book together with Poula Helth also dealing with protreptic. This was a great experience. To Allan Holmgren, great therapist and dear friend I want to express my gratitude too. Also to Professor Jan Molin who opened his executive education to protreptic. To the people around The Centre of Art & Leadership of which I am the director I also want to express my gratitude, especially to Professor Pierre Guillet de Monthoux, Professor Rob Austin, to Soeren Friis Moeller and to Helle Hedegaard Hein, and to the conductor Peter Hanke, who built the centre together with me, and to the violinist Karen Humle, who I met only recently.

The trust yielded to me by the former leader of CBS, Finn Junge-Jensen has formed the rock on which we all stand when we try dangerous new ventures. I also owe a thank you for their support of the project to the former director of LPF, Eva Zeuthen Bentzen, and to my very close friend and, I would say, "mentor", Henrik Hermansen, who has co-developed Center of Art & Leadership and, with his never failing sense of the important and his eminent strategic talents, generously supported my ideas. Great support too, in different ways, and lots of inspiration, was given to me by my friend, the instructor Bent Noergaard. My dear friend Professor Emeritus Ole Dybbroe, who died last year, always guided and supported me through a lifetime in spite of his comprehensions as to my political realism, he shall also be mentioned here. He will never be forgotten.

My publishers Henrik Schjerning, Lise Nestelsø and Anne Weinkouff deserve appreciation of their solidarities with my projects.

However, much gratitude must also be given to all the people who in spite of their vulnerable singularity dared to do protreptic conversations with me before a public sometimes consisting of up to 500 people.

Prologue

It is some ten years since I discovered protreptic. What still amazes me is that it was I who apparently rediscovered it as a practice in relation to management. Viewed from the perspective of therapy it shares a part of its theoretical optics, its attitudes, and its "method" with the philosophical counselling-program developed by Leonard Nelson, with the attempts to develop the Socratic dialogue, and with existential therapy. However its roots are first and foremost the classical Greek philosophy and Stoicism. It grew out the Greek ideal of permanent education, the "paideaia".

I estimate that in the last four years I have undertaken around 500 protreptic sessions with one or a few more persons in front of an audience in a corporate- or university-setting. To this must be added the sessions conducted with one person only in a room with the doors shut.

Considering that times have changed since antiquity, I had to develop protreptic so that it could match the demands of changed personal identities, new and transformed modes of communication, and new types of problems, especially the ones of organizations, private or public, raised by the urgent demand of making values real.

Protreptic is a very old philosophical art. It was created by the Greeks 400 B.C. by philosophers and rhetoricians and finished in its form around 320 B.C.

It is connected with famous names like Plato, Aristotle, and Isocrates and Epicurus. Its influence was considerable both because it was the foundation of the education, mentoring and consulting of the prince, and because, after Gutenberg, it shaped the guidelines for addressing the public about matters of the good life. In Neo-Stoicism during the baroque it was the motor in an often rather profane upsurge of moral sentiment as a pendant to the religious reformism dominating Europe until the Enlightenment, the French Revolution and the Napoleonic wars changed everything.

The protreptic which I present to you here owes much to the Greek thought, a fact also emphasized by the role played by the Stoics in my theory of the event. However, despite the immense debt we owe to them and to the Romans who inherited their philosophy and rhetoric, we cannot reproduce the Greek mindset, since we live in another world. That is why I speak about the "new protreptic". One cannot invent a concept twice, but just because protreptic was originally a program for educating leaders, before it became a discipline of mastering one's own life directed to a broader public, there is no need to feign that exactly the former task is unimportant today, when it is the "pharmakon" which the world cries for. In other words, the Greek already knew.

The Greek appeal to the four core values, the good, the just, the true and the beautiful has only changed its content a little bit, to which recent investigations by UNESCO on global values testifies. Of course sharia differs from the European sense of practicing the law, but in the USA death penalty exists, and China has still an inhuman way with criminals. However, the individual, ideal significations of these values might be shared by the population of the whole world, even if the practice defers.

Greek science has become obsolete, but today we live in a Greek way in relation to health, since their core instruments for obtaining health was motion and diet. In every organization the dialogue increases its importance, and dialogue was developed to such a refined degree in theory and practice by the Greeks that no recent theory of communication or semantics can compete with it. The canonical work of the second half of the last century on pragmatic communication "Theorie des kommunikativen Handelns" by Jürgen Habermas, cannot to my opinion compete with the psychological insights and conceptual keenness of the rhetoric tradition.

Today concepts of social and gender identity have changed, social structures have been transformed to an overwhelming degree, and in the wake of information technology new needs for, and new ways of, communication have arisen, and new theories of communication have been launched. New sciences have emerged, like psychology and sociology, and therapy and coaching has grown into an industry. The level of human understanding across classes has increased enormously through Christianity, and the family structure has changed, even if the levels of intimacy have not, and the Christian attitudes of life differ considerably from the Greek. Considering such reasons protreptic must be presented in a different way, with other emphases and partly with other goals too.

In the Greek executive academies, the pupils were princes and military leaders, people well acquainted with ruthlessness, and mercilessness and driven by the will to power, by desires for women, land and luxuries. They were people with strict codes of honor, and perhaps even hostile to the science of the soul. Today we meet others types of leaders in our executive academes coming from very different cultural contexts and normally women, even though the world is still prone to cruelty. We meet leaders who want to lead through understanding and gentleness and who want to create the basis of autonomy and initiative in their employees – even if this to a certain degree might be seen as a product of technologic and economic necessity and not just as a development in normative awareness for its own sake. They wish to develop capacities like empathy, giving recognition and creating trust, and they want to be respected as human beings, and not merely as managers.

But most important, I presume, is the immense growth in the general sense of the right to and the possibility of freedom in the global population, however different the social and economic conditions of its concrete implementation and fulfillment might be. And freedom is the goal and navigational technique of protreptic.

Different socio-economic settings call for new attitudes and concepts, but the Greek developed protreptic in its core. This must not be forgotten. However, we cannot imitate the Greek theory, because we cannot imitate their practice. So, what I present here is *my* version of protreptic, and should it be subject to criticism or even to blame, the fault is mine alone.

It must be stated at once: Nobody can take patent rights to protreptic. However there is a minimum level of conceptual precision and epistemological consequence defining the project. This was in its main structure developed by the Greeks and it cannot be dispensed with. From here we start again, trying to incorporate the best from modern philosophy, communication theory, pragmatics, ethics, and therapy.

The perspective of the new protreptic presented here is the one of phenomenology, because I am a phenomenologist, and its core meta-theory is the one of the event developed by me through the last ten years in my trilogy of the event, "Eventum tantum. The Ethos of the Event", "Beauty Happens. The Aesthetics of the Event", and "The Self Happens. The Event of Consciousness". They are, alas, all published in Danish.

Ever since Edmund Husserl, phenomenology programmatically distanced itself from psychology. So does my protreptic. But it would be foolish to deny that a successful protreptic session is built on – what one generally names – a "sense of psychology". As stated in the book this sense could be a sense of significance of the event and of the mind of the other, not the projection of models of desires or models of personalities and their reified qualities. If psychological sense is understood as the sense of the event and of the possibilities of the other person, protreptic is also a psychological practice.

There is no need to dig trenches. The protreptic session is always a place of learning for the protreptic guide himself and this openness must also characterize protreptic as a mini-paradigm.

1.

What is protreptic?

Thinking, called "diánoia" in his last dialogues, was defined by Plato as "entos tes psyches pros aúten diálogos", as "the inner dialogue of thought with itself"; the act of thinking, "dianoeist-hai" was seen as the same as "dialégesthai", as the mode of conversation, a prior form of dialectic (Sophist 263, e 3-5; Theaitetos 189 e). This is the epistemic basic assumption of protreptic: that thinking and speaking are two sides of the same coin. By guiding speech in the right way, one might learn to think in the right way, and vice versa.

The concept of protreptic is found in the culture of Athens from 400 B.C. and onwards. It is used by Plato, and his opus could be considered as protreptic in character, as an experiment in "para-inesis", the art of turning another person to philosophy as a way to manage one's own life. Plato's devotion to the Socratic "euprat-tein", the "ethically mastered" life, and his obligation towards the examination of the self, makes his attitude protreptic. He also speaks in the "Sophist" about the art of "techne psychagogia", the art of guiding the soul of the other person. However, it was Aristotle whose most important, esoteric work was the "Protrep-tikos logos", the admonition to do philosophy. It was Aristotle who created an executive program for leaders around the middle of the fourth century B.C. on the Island of Cypern, sponsored by the king Themiston.

On the basis of the magnum opus of Aristotle we can define protreptic as *dialectic applied with the aim of prompting a person to liberate himself by reflecting on her/his basic values.* Thus protreptic is bound to social dialogue, and to the possibility of becoming the master of one's own inner dialogue.

Aristotle's famous presentation of the true forms of argument, the "logic", put forward in "Prior Analytics" and in "Posterior Analytics", and all the tricks by which one rejects the Sophists described in the "Topics" and in the "On Sophistical Refutations", are all protreptic studies. The The famous "Art of Rhetoric" can be seen as another contribution to the protreptic art, because non-manipulative rhetoric *IS* protreptic. One of the arenas for refuting the Sophist is a sort of dialogical duel before an audience, and this is a scenario referred to by Aristotle in his presentation of the eristic models of argumentation.

Of course the first focus on the dialogue was above all pro-jected by Plato and his alter ego, Socrates, and Plato is the father of dialectic and of the fourfold distinction used in discussion, which Aristotle presents to us in the beginning of "On Sophis-tical refutations". "Didactic (didaskalikoi), Dialectical (dialek-tikoi), Examinations-arguments (peirastikoi), and Contentious arguments (eristikoi)" (II, 1, 165b), all go back to the branch of Plato's "system" described by Diogenes Laertius in his "Lives of Eminent Philosophers" as the part defined by "zetikos", searching. It involves the "agonistikos", containing "endeiktikos" (criticizing), and the "anatreptikós" (refuting) on the one side, and the "gym-nastikòs" (training of mental capacities) on the other side, covering the "maieutikós" (the mental delivering), and the "peirastikós" (the self-criticizing), (I, iii,49). Aristotle claims that the "to gymnasion" is the first of the three purposes of investigating dialectic in his "Topica", the other two being "enteuzis" (conversation) and the philosophy of science, a concept with no other equivalent than the concept of true knowledge "episteme" which would also encompass the meta-level suggested by the modern phrasing "philosophy *of* science".

Protreptic, like all Greek philosophy, is directed towards one goal: "... for all things pursue pleasure and desire it for its own sake;" as Aristotle would put it in the Rhetoric (I,vii,22, Loeb Edition). What gives pleasure is the good, and the good is that which "everything if possessed of practical wisdom, (phronesin) would choose." This is the good, "which is desirable for its own sake and not for anything else" – and this is pleasure. In the text Aristotle uses "hedoné" for pleasure, but most often he would use the word "eudaimonia", a pleasure combining the physical and the intellectual joy, both in "The Art of Rhetoric" (I, iv, 5), and in the "Nicomachean Ethic".

Now, protreptic is the art of knowing what pleasure is, and how we acquire it. And since pleasure is the opposite of pain the real pleasure must be of a kind which is not followed by pain. This is the pleasure of doing and thinking the good, and this is the general concept of Plato.

What is special of protreptic in relation to ethical dialectic in general is only that it is a discipline that from its origin is directed towards leaders. It is the system of knowledge about how one teaches the leader to pursue happiness as a leader, and the conclusion is always given: he must search in the capacity of a human being. But since he is especially tempted by the misuse of power, desires for luxury, for women, etc., he must be particular on guard in relation to his own values of life. His life must, so to speak, be an extra-examined one. This is why protreptic was called "to soften the tyrant", but also "the mirror of the king", or "the king's road". The dialogue of protreptic creates a mirror for the other unique person only, in which he would be able to see who he really is, and see the one he could become if he acts out of virtue. It is closely related to a concept of adult education, or "executive education", as we would say today, and one famous educator, Isocrates, a contemporary of Plato, would – as Cicero said – have produced as many leaders during his long life "as there were Greeks in the Trojan horse". Werner Jaeger did not give us the same denigrating picture of Isocrates as a sophist as Plato and his followers were inclined to (the references are often partly concealed, though), but instead underlined Isocrates' nationalistic perspective so dominant after the devastating Peloponnesian Wars between Athens and Sparta (431-404). The intimate connection between protreptic and rhetoric is documented by the fame of Isocrates as a speech writer – he did not perform the speeches himself due to lack in the power of his voice or to his timidity.[1]

If we jump forward 2500 years, the protreptic message to the modern leader becomes one of self-reflection: The more he examines his own life, the more he can convince through integrity, authenticity, and an authoritative presence. However, he might also

---

1 Werner Jaeger: Die Formung des griechischen Menschen. Berlin, New York: Walter de Gruyter 1989.

assist in the examining of others' lives, especially his employees. From this perspective protreptic transmutes from being the art of admonishing the would-be tyrant, to the "ruler's art" of helping other people to acquire freedom of mind. For that is the gift of protreptic: A life based on the liberty of knowing one's own values, and of the capacity to critique whatever is pressed upon us as the truth of our own lives, by internal desires or external mores. The primary picture is no longer Nero killing his protreptic adviser Seneca – he actually ordered him to kill himself – for cautiously telling him how to direct his life, but Nero trying to understand what his people really want by inviting them to dialogue. Hence, protreptic today could be a gesture of symmetry.

The word protreptic has the root "trépo" or "tropein": to turn, which is kept in the concept of "trope" and "trópos": a turn or direction, way, mores, form of life, character, attitude, or meaning. And trope means solstice, victory, defeat, change. In the New Testament Mary is converted to a totally new life by the empty grave, when she turns around and sees Christ, and the verb used here, "epistrephein", is translated by St. Augustine to "converto/conversio": to change confession – a concept hidden in the word "conversation", a dialogue which might change one's views and attitudes.

It is a function of the overall Greek philosophical program of "epimeleia heautou", the "cura sui", the care of oneself for the sake of one's Self.

However, it is also led by the principle of the good rhetoric, stated thus by Aristotle:

"... for as a matter of right, one should aim at nothing more in speech than how to avoid exciting pain or pleasure." (Rhe. III, i, 5.) One should facilitate the insight of the other person into himself, and if this gives pleasure, this is due to the structure of the mind. If it should be the primary goal, this originates in the ideal of "eudaimonia", the union of intellectual and physical wellbeing.

16

2.

Why protreptic

The reasons why a forgotten tradition suddenly becomes important can be found in the socio-economic setting. The pressure on management to transform into leadership, the public surveillance of organizations and their increasing dependence on their stakeholders, especially employees, but also on customers as co-producers and co-innovators, demands new approaches to communication through dialogues. The increasing power of the enlightened and critical, or even, political, consumer demands new types of leadership. TV reinforces the strange phenomenon that an effective speaker always addresses each individual in a crowd – even if they, as a consequence, act as a mass – and thus simulates a peculiar form of the dialogical form. Every person must feel that he, and especially he, is addressed. TV did that because the possibilities of answering back often are formally non-existent or postponed and carried over to other media (though the blog and face book phenomena produced by the internet have changed this heavy non-reciprocity and diminished the power of the lack of simultaneity).

In the wake of the increase of so called 'intimate technologies'—e.g., value based management, management by passion, formal and informal recognition, and by coaching—the dialogical capacities of management have to be intensified in the direction of an ideal of symmetry, if they are to function with a self-secure and highly educated workforce. It is here protreptic becomes newly interesting, and in order to understand the full range of its potential influence, we have to look closer at the new conditions of management and organizing.

A remark: The reader may already at this early stage object, why another technology of dialogue when therapy and coaching are invading almost any context? The answer shall come in the course of the presentation of protreptic, but it can be stated at once that protreptic is neither another therapy nor a refined form of coaching. Protreptics deals with values only, and values are anonym. It is not a contribution to increase the labyrinth of self-biography through yet another construction of an "ego". It is a way to recreate the the self by understanding that its core is shared with anyone else. The most general is the most personal.

3.

The new problems of leading and organizing

The problems of the new leadership are many:

1. The increasing role of stakeholders, consumers, suppliers, employees, and open innovation.
2. The demand of co-production of public service by the citizen.
3. The growth of corporate obligations towards society and towards stakeholders.
4. The criteria and methods of private business begin to form the content of political planning and evaluation of the public sector, and shape management and organization in this sector.
5. The enormous increase in the role of employees as a form of capital.
6. The dominance of immaterial work.
7. The increase in the role of relation-forming and networking inside and among firms as a means to innovation, intensification of work, creation of new markets, and overall growth.
8. The increasing demand of qualified labor at an elite-level.
9. The problems of recruiting and keeping virtuoso-employees.
10. The demand for leading employees who are expected to lead themselves.
11. New intimate technologies for leading and organizing.
12. Demands usurping the whole life of the worker appropriating his intellectual, emotional, and conative forces, his passion, engagement and creativity.
13. The need to solve the work-life tension produced by this usurpation and appropriation.
14. The demand to create corporate selves at a new, virtual level.

Looking back on history, first and foremost the Catholic Church, the military and the classical bureaucracy of the Prussian character succeeded in creating corporate selves, but also some enterprises with long lives managed to do this, like the Danish Maersk. They were dominated by compact value systems, basic loyalty, mutual trust, and firm codes of conduct, and by a solidarity at the horizontal level, which was not critical towards the organization, and towards leadership – the opposite attitude often being characteristic of both the skilled and unskilled industrial workers in for example car industries and shipbuilding yards, and in all enterprises using masses of workers and assembly lines.

Today this is seldom possible, because employees, to an increasing degree, are most loyal to their CVs, and because the knowledge-based character of work implies differentiations, and thus both blocks solidarity, and makes loyalty to the firm delicate, even when management acts through individualization of recognition and rewards. Teamwork does not, counter-intuitively, seem to produce sufficient incentives to create deeper solidarity among employees, probably due to its intermediary and trans-disciplinary form, and due to the competition between employees. Yet there are exceptions. Microsoft was awarded the prize for the Greatest Place to Work for two years in Denmark on the basis of the personal-politics, and the satisfaction of the employees. Let's take a look at it.

At Microsoft all workers are presented with the need for engagement, passion, and commitment. They are immediately presented with the problem of work-life-balance, especially stress – on the very first day they are admonished not to overwork, and are taught about the prevention of stress through lectures and workshops, and life-work-balance is built into all HR processes. They are offered great flexibility and challenged to use it, and they are urged to effectuate self-management. There are monthly conversations with management. The HR department checks whether the managers do conduct the staff development interview. The harmonization or attunement of expectations is carefully produced through the employee's acceptance of a set of commitments which form the basis of a running evaluation of his performance. The new man in Microsoft is obliged to take some courses, which he must pass in order to continue in the firm. He is also required to undertake further education. Taken together, these educational arrangements are called (readiness-activities), and it exists as a computer program, Role Guide, through which any employee is able to develop his own educational plan based on his own commitments. There are a lot of perks. Children are allowed at work, bicycles can be repaired, e-shopping can be done, and food brought in.

The buzz word of management is "self-management". This can be cut down to the conflicting demands to accomplish the contracted tasks and not to overwork at the same time.[2] Self-management is often defined as the opportunity for the employee to set his own immediate goals, and to attune them to the goals of the organization, while at the same time attempting to deepen these goals or even change them, but only under a permanent self-guiding evaluation of this harmonization.[3] It has the ring of a self-demand to do something which one even does not know that one is able to. That this is done in the interest of the firm is secured through a manifold strategy of building a corporate personality, which embodies an intrinsic motivation, which ideally should grow infinitely.

Researchers have underlined a transition from normative to neo-normative control, from the attempt to create a corporate identity of the employee to the attempt to control his autonomy.[4] Other writers have emphasized the emerging of new behavioral and mental forms of resistance, among others cynicism as a reaction to the intimate technologies.[5] What characterizes these diagnoses is the fact that both managerial strategies and the reactions of the employees are individual, no collective resistance is built.

However, it is worth mentioning that its employees seem to be very happy about working with Microsoft, and the firm seems actually to take really good care of the workers when one observes

---

2 See: Computerworld 2008, 21-11, Vekommen til Windows Woderland). Lederne, Du skal undgå at arbejde for meget. 2008, 15-8). Berlinske Nyhedsmagasin, topmøde om arbejdsglæde 16-11, 2007.
3 Authors have stressed the so-called "bio-politics" as a way to integrate the life of the employee into work. See: Lazzarato, M. (2004): From Capital-Labour to Capital-Life. *Ephemera*, 4 (3).
4 Fleming, P. & Spicer, A. (2007): Just be yourself – Towards neo-normative control in organizations.
5 Contu, A. (2008): Decaf Resistance: On misbehavior, cynicism and desire in a liberal work-place. *Management Communication Quaterly* 21 (3), pp. 364-79.

them from within the firm. Tacit resistance does not appear to be a problem in this work-place. This might confirm bio-politics as a perspective, but it might also reject its negative sides.

Self-management is not only a clever form of control, even if it sounds so, but can be seen in the light of the Greek philosophical legacy in which the technique of the self called "epimeleia heautou", in Latin "cura sui" to take care of oneself as a self, has an important place. The concept originates with Plato but its significance is increased in Stoicism, and generally through the Hellenistic philosophy and the Romans incorporation of this great tradition in their eclectic mode of usurping foreign traditions. It should be mentioned that Michel Foucault focused on the "cura sui" during Hellenism in his "History of Sexuality" in his development of the concept of bio-politics. The management of the self presupposes an understanding of what the self might possibly be, and this is the subject of protreptic together with the development of the means to approach this self and realize it. But protreptic is never a procedure for hire by the firm; rather, its only goal is to exhort the singular person to liberate himself.

The branding ideology of Microsoft is overwhelming: "We let you love what you love at work". "Whatever you choose to become, we let you become more of it". "Microsoft donates $17 for every hour you volunteer."[6] Or, as international corporate manager Steve Balmer states, "I love this company. You should love this company."[7]

This way of speaking is rather new, and does not match Danish mentality. But an announcement from a Microsoft employee like the following could be found anywhere:

> *"There was this instance where I got a great idea and I actually came in at three in the morning, because I couldn't sleep. I had to start cutting up this idea that I had thought of, right. We just believe in this and wanna put everything into it..."*[8]

---

6   www. Youtube.com/watch?v 1rXbAY8qHvg.
7   1: www. Youtube.com/watch?v = vwsboPUjrGc,
8   www.Youtube.com/watch?v = XckRq4m2uM.

One could speak about a type of empowerment which has a virtual character since it implies that the employee never has done enough.

The top manager of Microsoft Denmark, J. Bardenfleth, says in an interview:

"In MS DK we have a performance culture, and the employees go far in order to reach their goals. We offer the workers so much leeway to plan their work themselves within the teams. We believe that by doing so we strengthen the employees' belief in that they themselves are the best ones to know how the tasks are solved. And here we are deep inside the implicit faith. It creates engagement and the will to reach the goals. The management at the same time has the responsibility of a mutual harmonization of expectations between the manager and the employee that they shall make priorities, be able to say no, and relieve the pressure, when work becomes too overwhelming. This is one of the reasons why we were elected the best place to work last year."[9]

What, however, is actually new here?

Jobs are described rather meticulously, and this description is reinforced individually through a list of commitments to which the employee must give his agreement. He shall probably not be able to influence the total list of commitments, but he might be involved in the deliberations on which ones are chosen. The enterprise has a set of values, and the profile of the ideal worker is outlined.

Precisely like any job in the church or the military, the bureaucracy and the higher level of employee work in private companies could be described since the 18th century. What differs is only the frankness with which the employee is able to function in the dialogue of these issues, but not his power. Probably also meetings with the department or top managers are now more frequent, and the practice of recognition more careful, more informal and colloquial, but in any of the mentioned systems in which there were firm criteria and strict procedures of promotion, both a running

---

9   Berlinske Tidende 28-9 2008 "Ledelse på spidsen"

evaluation of the performance of the employee and the reckoning of a sum total each year would be a norm.

Also an extreme focus on individual performance was to be found; and consistent with that a process of "subjectivation", the goal of which is to shape the employee.

What has shifted is that far more people have a higher status in the organization than earlier due to the knowledge based character of work, and that in some occupations innovation is sought for. This makes "subjectivation" far more difficult today. However, when East Germany still existed, statistics were produced each year to document the innovative capacity of the workers, summing up to one million. Evaluation of innovative performance is not anything new. Disney practiced this many years ago. It cannot be denied that McGregor's famous distinction between x-factors and y-factors shows a change in managerial practices in industry, but they have for centuries been an obvious attitude towards officers, priests, higher bureaucrats, and CEOs.

What's really differentiates the branding ideology is the fact that much work in industry has been able to satisfy desires for using more mental capacities, and for individual influence on the performance of tasks through increased responsibility. Many organizations have come to resemble very firmly controlled universities.

Looking at old Danish firms like Maersk, ØK, the Danish Bank, and more recent ones like Danfoss and Grundfos, the lives at the level of local line leaders and above, of engineers and of researchers have not changed considerably. Most employees in these firms have always done "immaterial work". There are definite, corporate identities of employees, and firm codes of conduct, creating dedicated and controlled personalities embodying the invisible values of the organization, even if the range and intensity of sanctions cannot match that of the old organizations and institutions. What is new in Business are the internal academies of leadership – the military and the church had them for centuries – and great educational programs. Thus the control of identity can never reach the earlier authoritative level.

However, dialogues have become more important in organizations due to the fact that employees are raised in an atmosphere in which authorities are questioned due to the overall prevalence of democratic practices. Orders are not as rational as requests or the designing of frames, since the employees are expected to accomplish tasks which cannot be defined precisely. Also the classical, hostile relations between workers and management have gone away since the employees do not experience themselves as a group, and do not rely on trade unions, but being knowledge workers often tend their egos and individual careers.

The IT-revolution has had an important role in individualizing workers by the creation of many new, and different job functions, and by blurring their mutual positions through the looser relations in rapidly changing teams and projects. So, the dialogues become more vertical and more individual, presupposing a common interest between the employee and the firm, far beyond the classical one of keeping the factory going. One does not talk to the boss in the capacity of a member of a group, not to mention a "class", but as a person who might be privileged if he plays his hand well.

From this perspective a firm like Microsoft is actually a new-technology firm with a very old form of organization, one supplied with some new fringe benefits or perks and a new type of corporate ideology, but also with a much more differentiated interest in the single employee.

It is interesting that firms like Maersk and the others mentioned above simply expected that an employee would have an ordered and proper private life, and so does Microsoft. No doubt these firms would articulate this to the employee at the beginning of their transaction, and it was the more easy to accomplish, since most employees began very young. What they would not do was use words like "stress" or "work-life-balance", but they would certainly demand that a task be done, and they expected it to be done after working hours, if it hadn't been accomplished. So they actually demanded a certain family structure. The pressures on Microsoft employees cannot be compared to the pressure laid on employees in the Danish ministries just now – the recent, terrifying results of the evaluation of the psychic work environment in the Ministry of Environment shows that. But in firms like Microsoft we have a far more intimate focus on the private life of the employee, which is not found in public administration.

The point is that the employees must learn to say "no", and to legitimate this. Such an attitude demands the capacity to refer to personal values on behalf of the employee, and the capacity of the leader to understand them, and this is where protreptic comes in. Perhaps basic values of organizations are not negotiable, but they need certainly to be interpreted at a level of mutual symmetry.

During the last years coaching has become the new type of intimate technology, and this is a new phenomenon, especially when the manager himself coaches. The asymmetry of this relation is obvious, and it is here protreptic becomes a valid alternative focus on values, not on personal qualities and individual life stories.

4.

The rules of protreptic

In the Greek the "protrepo" also means "to confront with (gently but insisting)", "to urge".

The subject of its result, the ideal protreptic dialogue, should accomplish a mental turning around, an insight into our innermost norms, ideals, attitudes, notions, thoughts, and practices, items worthy of aspiring to, in relation to the leader's and the employee's ethical development, their sense of the mutual and the possible, and their responsibility towards the community.

Protreptic is an art. It is a calling for philosophy, a license to think, both with the intellect, and with the heart.

The protreptic guide does not orientate himself – contrary to the therapist, mostly – in relation to a "naturalistic conception", in relation to an idea about how a person, a leader, a group or an organisation ought to be, or act. It aims at a balance between pleasure and insight, to refer to the dialogue "Philebus" by Plato, to a balance between strategic instrumentality and normativity. It seeks an ethical canon beyond maxims, and an attitude almost immune to pragmatics. It is never moralizing.

The goal of the protreptic guide is to enable the leader to articulate the principles of individual and collective freedom.

The assumption of the protreptic guide is that man and the organisation are shaped in the image of each other, and that it is possible to create an unambiguous reason for individual and organisational behaviour based on the ideal of the Good and the Just.

Protreptic claims that an existential code does exist through which the differences and contradictions of interests between members of a community, and hence, of an organisation, can be reconciled. But protreptic knows that there is a price. The price is to negate any concept of the rational agent by invoking a greater rationality than the conservatio sui, a rationality which put the value and idea over personal pleasure and even survival, but never at the cost of other people's suffering. Proteptic is as far from an ideology as it is possible to imagine.

Protreptic shows a way to discover the original face of the other person. The intentional attitude of this discovery is one of respect. This respect for the face of the other person de-limits the right to project motives and attitudes onto the other person. It must not be forgotten that most influential theories of ideal, caring and careful communication, as known from the work of Martin Buber and Emmanuel Lévinas, have a religious basis. Instrumentality and strategy of communication are challenged by protreptic in the name of love.

Protreptic re-discovers the ability to listen to the voice of the other, whether it is silent or loud (I say "re"-discover because the Stoic made the art of listening into a virtue). As far as the voice is naked, we must cover it with modesty, and even with shyness. We must guard the secret of the Other.

Protreptic has its rules and proclivities, but not any dogmatic ones. They are:

1. Putting into words the existential attitudes to life and work, to individual rights and duties, to normatively based personal expectations at all levels of life, and to a balanced relation between competencies and professionalism.
2. To create a consciousness about notions, prejudices, proto-typical projections, and intentional anticipations which block personal development, the understanding of the other person, and the responsible integration into the community.
3. The development and strengthening of a fundamental, critical sense, by opening new modes and depths of self-reflection.
4. The full consciousness of the fundamental importance of the event to every little movement in our lives, and hence, of the line of demarcation between that which is in our power, and that which is not.
5. The ability to adhere to a personal ideal of the creation of an inner harmony through ethical development.
6. The surmounting of psychological reductionism, and the development of a creative empathy. To be able to experience

through substantiated scepticism, through just indignation, and through trust and generosity.

7. The strengthening of an ethical imagination.

8. The replacement of strategic communication directed at persuasion, seduction, and the control of attitudes, with the respect of the singularity and autonomy of the other person: Leadership as never ending discovery. The humour and irony of the private detective must replace the obstinate seriousness of the inquisitor and superintendent. Together we must discover our common cause, the core of the process of organising.

9. The development of a concept of personal formation as the basis of the loops of learning, and not the least of the strategies for forgetting. To be able to unite professionalism, passion, and will, through an ideal of the transformation of functions, tasks, procedures, domains of responsibilities, and criteria of excellence.

10. The lack of any firm institutional frame. The protreptic can take place everywhere, between everybody, and all the time. It is direct, quiet, sober, sensitive, serious, and not without humour.

11. Protreptic deepens the concept of self-management both critically and supportively by developing the sense of self in the other person.

In order to understand the full range of the protreptic approach, we must have a closer look into the epistemology and ontology which it presupposes.

5.

A model of the self

Most people with whom I have spoken about the architecture of our inner, mental space would agree on two structural aspects: That we have an internal, three-dimensional space even if the principles of time governing it might differ from linear time (as both Henry Bergson and Edmund Husserl suggested); and that the self consists of at least two inner voices. The first aspect is anticipated by many metaphorical expressions like "the labyrinth of the mind", "the stream of consciousness", "the subliminal level", "that beneath the threshold of consciousness", "the subconscious domain". "The subconscious" is a much older concept than Freud's, and was already elaborated by the time he takes hold of it, among others by Johann Friedrich Herbart, and the Romantic Movement. "Subconscious" was used by Thomas de Quincy for the first time in English in 1823, "preconscious" emerged in 1860, and philosophers like Arthur Schopenhauer and Eduard Hermann explored the unconscious. Other metaphors are "the depth of the mind" (the oldest sense of "mind" being "memory"), "layers, levels, rooms of the mind", "exploring your emotional depths", and witnessed by for example Buddhism when one speaks about the clear sky of the mind. Language also corroborates the second structure by phrases like "speaking to oneself", "lie to oneself", "my better self", etc., and it is already anticipated by the word "consciousness", where the "con-", "the together with," implies more than one agent – the Greek concept "syn-eidesis" or Danish "sam-vittighed" have the same content. Freud's famous model of consciousness with its distinction between an Id, an Ego, and a Superego, suggests that too. In several dialogues Plato already defined thought as an inner dialogue. And Arthur Schnitzler's and James Joyce's contributions to literature explore the inner dialogues – their characters Leutnant Gustl and Fräulein Else and Leopold Bloom speak to themselves.

From this perspective there would be an "I-1" interpreting and expressing the primary mental functions from direct experience of the world via desires, emotions, motives, intentions and interests, to knowledge, lines of thoughts, and memories. I-1 is able to articulate itself through four dimensions: Discursive language (inner speech – "logos endiathetos" in Stoic vocabulary); remembered events, structured and listed as "situations", or unstructured; mental images; and inner intensities like desires, urges, passions, emotions, states of mind. At the level of I-1 the sensing of the world is also transformed into descriptions, rebuilt into information, or presented as demands, wishes, and also as the imitated voice of others.

The important insights of Henri Bergson in "Memory and Matter" can guide us here. It identifies the capacity of action as the core of perception thus denying a special non-dynamical storage of mental images, and emphasizing the role of the whole body in experience:

> *"The progress by which the virtual image realizes itself is nothing else than the series of stages by which the image gradually obtains from the body useful actions or useful attitudes. The stimulation of the so-called sensory centers is the last of these stages: It is the prelude to a motor reaction, the beginning of the action in space."*

and

> *"Between the intention, which is what we call pure memory, and the auditory memory-image properly so called, intermediate memories are commonly intercalated which must first have been realized as memory-images in more or less distant centers."*[10]

Thus Bergson is able to create a concept of intentionality very different from the one developed by Edmund Husserl by focusing on the active role of the body, a perspective later to become so crucial to such eminent thinkers as Maurice Merleau-Ponty, Michel Foucault, and Gilles Deleuze. Memory is working in every

---

10 Henri Bergson: *Matter and Memory*. New York: Cosimo Classics. 1912/2007, p. 168 and 167.

perception which becomes an experience, and memory is the body's remembering of its own acts and reactions.

A theory of perception thus must operate with an active memory. Memories are stores as capacities for movement, since the propensity to act or to stop action, is exactly what is remembered as the sense of the memory. Since personal memories consist of stored events, these events must both be seen as shaped by the virtual action inherent in them, and they themselves as subject to permanent transformation. In any event this propensity to act goes back to actual action remembered, or back to virtual action, of course also implying the lack of capacity, opportunity or will to act, due to lack of courage, fear of pain, but also due to disinterestedness. Behind such a propensity there always lies a value, since every act can be referred back to one or more basic values, and to – what could be called – "inferred", "intermediate", or "situated" values.

So the speech of I-1 has a mood. This mood, however, is not really established or articulated consciously until the other inner voice has spoken. This would be an "*I-2*" representing the capacity of reflecting on the content of I-1, and with a special outlet to the realm of values. This presupposes most of the time that I-1 operates through discursive articulation, even if you can relate to semantic entities of a non-discursive character, like in plastic remembrances of events, of faces, sequences of actions, or dreams, or – canonically – through the mood of bad conscience or guilt.

The timbre or color of I-2 might not differ from the one of I-1 – although as the one reproaching, admonishing or advising, it might use a more firm or serious voice—but its function certainly does. I-2 asks *why* I-1 proceeds in the way it does. Far back in history, but more recently by Immanuel Kant, the court is used to illustrate this structure of mind provided with an accused, attorneys from the state and from the defense, and even with a judge or a jury. Plato on his side uses another metaphor in his last dialogue, "The Laws", namely the one from war, where the I-1 is at war with I-2, and the latter needs to win over I-1 in order that the self might feel free.

However the existence of two voices presupposes a third instance, something which guarantees that the experience of the difference is not a mere projection of each of the "I's". The difference between the two "I's" forms a relation-shaped being present for some third unit which experiences or registers their activity. This third instance I call *the Third I.* This third I is often referred to as a knowledge of the fact that thought takes place, i.e. as an assurance of an inner sense-generation; but it is also sensed as a feeling of an inner witness, a mirror, or even a judge. It is the presence of mind as presence. Through it alone some certainty can be obtained.

Many philosophers, but Immanuel Kant and J.G. Fichte in particular, underline the fact that the Third I cannot be of a discursive nature, because this would produce an infinite regression of "I's". J. G. Fichte is extremely lucid in his argumentation here. Hence, the Third I cannot sense data, since this presupposes the linguistic activity of an I-structure, but has to experience at another level. I call this level the *sensing by significance.*

This sensing by significance describes a process which conceives of everything in an event at the level of significance, which means that it perceives beyond representation and denotation, i.e. beyond the sign. It has no substantial character even if it might produce an echo, but this is lost in our inner universe like a dense fug, oozing into the Third I as into a huge opening, a horizon, an abyss. It answers to a shared basic knowledge of the space of our own mind, of something lying beyond the realm of discourse, and not just beyond the realm of what we know that we know, but even beyond that which we do not know that we know (but might come to know, or never shall be able to word); it is beyond the tacit dimension of knowledge. If we make the distinction between knowing that we know something, knowing that we do not know something, and not knowing that we know *something, the sense of significance is* often situated at this last level. However in the capacity of mood it might be transformed into a subject of reflection, even if it cannot be directly articulated, but has to use metaphors and similarities like poetry does in order to be expressed.

Then, in a certain sense of knowing, we definitely "know" at the level of significance. But perhaps we should substitute awareness for knowing here. The sensing by significance forms a state of consciousness equal to the one produced by the relation between I-1 and I-2, though it has quite another character. It is always present through *the principle of translocutionarity*: When I hear myself thinking or speaking, I recognize something at work in these processes of sense production. This can never be directly articulated; even if we for example are inclined to identify it with a feeling of shame or unjustified hostility already immediately in the process of thinking or speaking, it is not the sensed significance proper. Due to the principle of translocutionarity we always have awareness of far more than we put into words.

The principle of translocutionarity says:

I do not know what I mean until I hear what I myself am saying.
I do not know what I do until I experience myself doing it.
I do not know what I know until *we* experience ourselves performing it.

This means that the event is the place in which I recognise myself in the capacity of another – to quote Paul Ricoeur. In the end knowledge refers to a collective process.

I developed this perspective in my doctoral thesis "Event and Body-Mind. A Phenomenological-Hermeneutic Analysis" from 1994 within the framework of speech act theory which denotes the fact that our understanding of our own thoughts, emotions, and intentions only become manifest when put into words in an event. Similar to the thousand years old adage of artists' reflection on their own creation of sense "I did not make the statue, I only liberated it from the stone", translocutionarity asks "How can I know what I mean until I hear myself say it?" This principle honours the role language has in inner dialogue, i.e. in overall mental activity, and hence its determining role for the concept of knowledge, but can be applied both to speaking and doing, and thus, to creativity, because the medium of expressions conveys sense, incorporates it, and forces us to take advantage of the immense realm of possibilities of meaning given through the medium. We discover what we actually did, thought, and felt by exploring the possible worlds of sense incorporated in our own product.

It is evident that memory also is stored by the different significance of its events. One might be inclined to think that the basic "grammar" of this language would be based on nuances of pleasure and pain, but this can only be half the truth. They are based on our registered capacity to act according to values. Thus stored events of accomplishment give pleasure, but this pleasure changes in accordance with the values, which it incorporates. The significance of a remembered event of generosity is different from a remembered event of the success by realising one's goals. The mood of liberation felt and freedom promised differs, because the act of generosity lasts forever, it does not need to be kept boiling, while the act of success must be repeated due to the demand for enforcement to keep its truth.

The connection between the Third I and the sensing of significance can be found epistemologically in the way in which the phenomenon of significance incorporates the being in the world, and the being one with it. The world as place, in the capacity of "chora",[11] transforms itself into the region of the mind, keeping its infinite shades of a sense beyond the sign.

The significance produced by the sensing of significance must not be conceptualized as an emotion. Emotions belong to the sphere of I-1 and I-2 both in the capacity of affects and passions, because they operate through the possibility of their discursive reproduction. Only through this are we able to handle them. Moods are more comprehensive, more all-pervading than emotions, and more difficult to articulate discursively, often due to the increasing poverty of linguistic equivalents – emotions might of course be too, but they have their vocabulary, as the list of sins and psychology's conceptual framework show.

Moods are knowledge-atmospheres, and they have a certain regressive character while we are inside them and are trying to word them, whilst we most often are able to stand back in relation to emotions. Hence, whole poems or musical works can be used capturing one complex mood, or to produce a new one, but their only relation to significance is to leave a trace.

Significance is something totally unique. It is not a mental object, neither is it a quality of the perceived outer world, nor of our inner realm. It is like a film drawn over the mental state hiding

---

11 The Greek concept "chora" is presented canonically by Plato in the "Timaeus". It means space, or place as the earth on which we are allowed to operate, because "chora" is a mother-like substance, opening her arms to us. I myself have been fascinated by this concept, and so have among others Jacques Derrida.

36

what it lets appear, as if it was its secret. Significance is the core of our feeling of the self, it operates through a terrifying and irrevocable intimacy. It is a overwhelming awareness, and it is always recognized as the fact of being in an event as "being evented": The relation is chiastic and transitive: A mind in a body, a body in an event, an event in a body, a body in a mind, a mind in an event, an event in a mind.[12]

The sensing by significance is the fingerprint of the eventing of the self; it points to a style of being. We have no proper words to grasp this mental process, but we are totally invaded by its impact, because it lies behind or "in" our deliberate decisions, i.e. in the capacity to will the will.[13] However, it must not be understood as a function of the "conservatio sui", of self-securing or self-promotion. It has nothing to do with the enlightened self-interest, with "the value for me" of what happens; rather, it refers to values beyond such values. These values of significance are transcendent and utterly personal in their appearance although they in general are shared, and hence, we cannot understand the sensing of significance as controlled by perspectives or as "paradigmatic". Anyhow, it is always present in everything we experience or do. So presence here means genuine presence, i.e. the presence of presence itself, and this presence is not present in the capacity of anything which is presented, and especially not an empirical ego or a substantial self.

I used the term "architecture" here in referring to the mind's space, but this is not precise if its connotations are a fixed state. Consciousness is an event of events, and self happens. Hence, self is neither a substance nor a subject. It is 'happened', so to speak.

The model of self presented here would look like this:

---

12 This primordial awareness might actually be what K.E. Løgstrup tried to express by his concept of the tuned state of mind. "Because significance lies beyond the familiarity of denotation and transcends it, to use a philosophical term, it is in the beginning unknown, only in a tuned state of mind we are open to it, but it has to be articulated first." "Kunst og erkendelse", p. 11.

13 In my opinion any thorough reflection on the phenomenon of the will shall reveal that it operates by a reflective but non-regressive structure presupposing that we can only will when we will our will to do something. This insight is a radical and important contribution of Hannah Arendt's work *The Life of the Mind*.

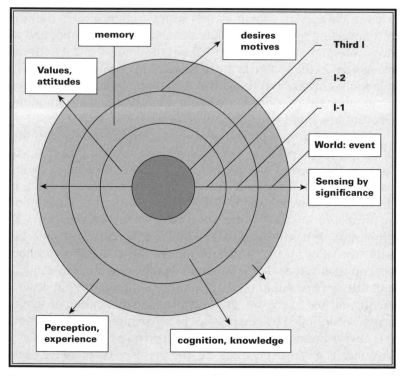

Figure 1. The mental space

The inner space could be seen as infinite. Take for example one remembered event, its possibilities of being interpreted are nearly endless in three aspects, because it exists as living color photography. Although it manifests itself in a finite form in the memory following the conditions posited by the minimum-level of perceptions, it has an absolute semantic infiniteness by the experience of actual and virtual agents already before its passage into memory, and as a reproduction of what 'really' happened in *my* memory it is subject to the work done by memory in relation to my enveloping perceptional existence in the events. If presented to others it might exist as second hand understandings as long as human beings exist to interpret and reproduce it; in principle it could form an endless series of causal and quasi-teleological lines in the life of other human beings, as it already accomplishes in me.

6.

The levels of perception

In order to complete this model of the self we have to consider the levels of perception.

We experience at four levels:

Level-1: At this level, I experience complexes in the world: forms, figures, movements, colors, often called "data", i.e. separate objects, their qualities, and the relations between them. In this capacity of perceiving I am "out in the world" primarily due to my sight, but also through the other senses – hearing is more often experienced from "a cave within" – but I am not directly or deliberately conscious of this consciousness as "a consciousness of something". The world there is given through the senses *as* sense impressions, often of a synthetic nature, combining all sense-activities with the capacity to move and touch – called "haptein" in Greek philosophy. Everything seems to hover in a dim "as-usual-ness". By this type of perception nothing else is revealed of the world than my being-right-there-in-it. It must not be mistaken for distraction, but the attention practiced by it is pragmatically unfocused. We could say that it is me who is being focused by the world, more than it is I who am doing the focusing. This type of perception does not need an "I", because it neither needs reflection nor even the separation of a subject from an object, which is needed for naming the process of perception as an event.

Language needs a tongue and hence a subject who uses it.

I call this level of perception *focusing without a subject.*

Level-2: The second level of perception makes perception itself an object. This does not necessarily imply an experience of an "I see that I see", because the process of seeing in relation to a seeing of this seeing only takes place when I know that I see; and a process of hearing and a hearing of this hearing only takes place when I know that I hear; and this process is the proper subject of conscious perception. Phenomenological philosophers like Maurice Merleau-Ponty called this level of perception a level of the "pre-reflective cogito", because although I am conscious of a world different from my body as part of this world, I am not yet conscious of this consciousness. This is a perception without concept, as Immanuel Kant baptized it, but it presupposes a sense of location, and hence of time and place.

At this level I relate to the world through action – or perhaps better, I "am related" by my action – an action not just automatic, but invested with a spontaneity in which goals might exist, because language is a part of it, but not deliberate goals, not planning, i.e. a reflective relation between means and ends.

If I want an apple lying on the ground I bend to pick it up, but I do not have to present this intention to myself, I know this is an apple, but no inner voice urges me to relate to it, it just happens with me, as if my body acted on my behalf having absorbed consciousness in its emerging intensity. Entangled bodies as in wrestling or in the act of love react in a similar way, but the spontaneity might arise, because quite a lot of contacts, grips, and touches, and caresses are not subject to language. The inner voice is forced to be silent, and even if the state of the body-mind should be an urge to increase force during wrestling this is more a state of being one with the body than an inner commentary. If rules of fighting should be needed they just present themselves as memories. Likewise the moving towards orgasm is knowledge in the body, not in the brain, unless it relates to the other person. Actually turning reflective consciousness on might ruin the whole process.

However, I know at a certain level the sense of the event and its contextual setting, but naming is superfluous during the process.

I am all in all present as a body, not as a mind. However, since we distinctly observe the difference between our body and that of the other, I shall call this mode of experience the mode of *practical reflectivity*.

I call this level of perception **subject-focused perception.** This is the first level to which we can subscribe experience, even if the subject is the body, or "the corporeal-complex-process", rather than an ego.

Level-3: The third level of perception involves the consciousness of an "I". We must know that we know *that* something is, and *what* it is; that is, we must be able to use language deliberately and reflectively in relation to it, and hence to say "I". To this type of perception cognition and hence discursive knowledge, is supplied, and thus it contains perspectives of experiencing and hence, a consciousness of the event-based mode of being. As Merleau-Ponty phrased it, the words are already out there with the objects.[14] The words pre-form the things and their relations to experience. In this capacity the thing is watching us through the optic of sense and the filter of words.

I call this mode of perception or experience ***I-focused experience.***

The first two levels of experience were dominated by I-1. The third level of experience contains I-2 also.

Level-4: The fourth level of perception I call **the sensing by significance.**

It is different from the three former levels by not using data and hence signs in the proper sense. It is formed by pervasive states, emotional states, by 'senses-of', by hunches, and the trans-reified character. It is neither bound to an explicit experience of a subject of perception detached from the world, nor is it discursive, and hence, bound to an "I".

The sense of the event is a product of the discursive activity of I-1, and I-2. The event of sense is only approachable by the sensing through significance, although this level is not its own creation. The perception at this level is related to the Third I. This relation is neither a result of intentionality – whether subjective or belonging to the language games – nor is it a quality inherent in the world itself. It is a genuine relation because it creates, and is created by, "a centre" (tó meson), an anonymous zone belonging to none of us, which happens.

---

14 The English translations of his major works are *Phenomenology of Perception*, trans. Smith, London: Routledge and Kegan Paul, 1962 (PP in text). *Sense and Nonsense*, trans. Dreyfus & Dreyfus, Evanston: Northwestern University Press, 1964 (SNS in text). *Signs,* trans. McCleary, Evanston: Northwestern University Press, 1964, and *The Visible and the Invisible*, trans. Lingis, Evanston: Northwestern University Press, 1968.

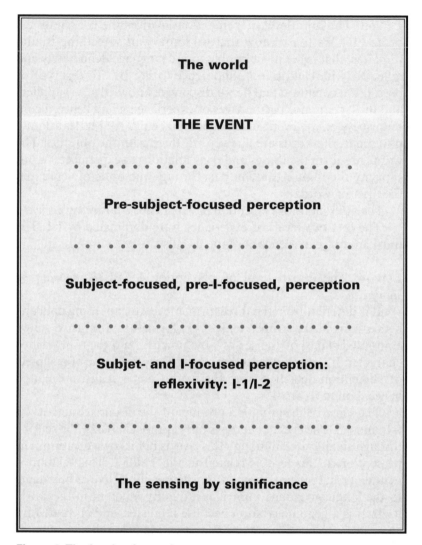

Figure 2. The levels of experience

My perception of my own inner reality by the Third I must have the same trans-objective, non-detached character as the one of the outer world. This perception is far more a kind of identification, a being one with the experienced more than a perception of something. We might use the word *mindful* or the expression *a-being-aware* – or even "being-awared".

We could form the hypothesis that the organization of memory follows principles inherent in the concept of sensing by significance, because the Third I absorbs the modes of speech between the two "Is" (representations of the "I"), about the remembered. But in spite of this appropriation of the practice or style of re-producing the ambiguous events of memory by the Third I we cannot allocate memory to the Third I, just as we cannot allocate desires and mental imagery, because it is not a type of container like the subconscious was supposed to be. This is caused by the fact that neither the sensing by significance nor the cognitive modes of the Third I operate through the sign. Rather the Third I is a hyper-consciousness.

This concept bears some resemblance to Merleau-Ponty's concept of "hyper-reflexivity" or "hyper-dialectic", but must not be confused with it. His idea is that philosophy in the capacity of a reflective discourse cannot catch the pre-reflective faith or reconstruct some pure immediacy:[15]

> *"What we propose here, and oppose to the search for the essence, is not the return to the immediate, the coincidence, the effective fusion with the existent, the search for an original integrity, for a secret lost and to be rediscovered, which would nullify our questions and even reprehend language. If coincidence is lost, this is no accident; if Being is hidden, this is itself a characteristic of Being and no disclosure will make us comprehend it".*[16]

In this capacity, a mode of thinking might be found that neither uses the sign nor discursive reflection:

> *"What we call hyper-dialectic is a thought that, on the contrary, is capable of reaching truth because it envisages without restriction the plurality of the relationships and what has been called*

15 "The Visible and the Invisible", p. 35, and p. 99.
16 Ibid. 121-122.

ambiguity. The bad dialectic is that which thinks it recomposes being by a thetic thought, by an assemblage of statements, by thesis, antithesis, and synthesis; the good dialectic is that which is conscious of the fact that every thesis is an idealization, that Being is not made up of idealizations or of things said… but of bound wholes where signification never is except in tendency" (VI 94).

Thus he propounds a dialectics beyond logic, and that idealization produced through our intercourse with it

"Abounds in the sensible world, but on condition that the sensible world has been divested of all that the ontologies have added to it. One of the tasks of the dialectic, as a situational thought, a thought in contact with being, is to shake off the false evidences, to denounce the significations cut off from the experience of being, emptied — and to criticize itself in the measure that it itself becomes one of them".[17]

Thus in a way the concept of sensing by significance is conceived as hidden in a situated non-logical 'dialectics' of the relation between the thinking and perceiving body and the world. However, the most important quality of this mode of experience is its non-linguistic character, and Merleau-Ponty was never able to decide definitively about the role of language in perception, sometimes giving it priority, sometimes nearly putting it into brackets. His untimely death never let him finish one of the greatest projects in European philosophy.

The present book holds the view that due to the character of the Third I, which can only be indirectly worded, there is no possibility of a genuine knowledge of oneself. We can approach our values, and our ways with them, but can get no further to the "secret guest", as Jean-Francois Lyotard called the self in his *Postmodern Fables.*

---

17 Ibid p. 92.

7.

The procedure of protreptic

Protreptic presupposes self-understanding through self-reflection and through self-examination. It is impossible to understand other persons without understanding oneself – an understanding which epistemologically can never be complete nor based on another certainty than the one actualized through the principle of translocutionarity, through one's acts, and through the speech acts which are always exposed to interpretation.

At the ontic level there exists a certainty which defies the knowledge of epistemology and the logic of science because it is needed as both a prologue and an epilogue to action. Certainty at a level strong enough to abolish the comprehensions about an action is necessary to activate the will, because we need a will to will, in order to intervene with the event. We all know that there is very often an ever so small doubt before an action, but this must be surmounted by decisiveness. We also must allow for the feeling of having acted well, or even done one's best, after the act. This certainty can never be absolute, but it is necessary if we should be able to realize the opposite.

We could state this otherwise by claiming that if there should be absolute certainty there would be no choice. Thus choice plays an enormous role in human affairs and certainly also in protreptic.

With the words of Soeren Kierkegaard we could say that one has to choose oneself.

The protreptic guide must urge the other person to choose himself. But this can, in the trans-psychological context of protreptic, only mean that one should choose one's own values, or leave them.

The way of protreptic, then, is to investigate the other person's internal space, i.e. the relations between his two "I's", and especially the character of the "Third I". because it is within the Third I that choice is generated.

This investigation can be undertaken in two ways. On the one side, one can make these structures and instances of the mind the direct subject of the dialogue by bringing in contextual questions like "What does it mean to be oneself?", "How do you know what is the best thing to do, when you face a normative dilemma?", or even "Who are you?". On the other side, one can indirectly consider the character of this inner state and its processes, constituted by the events of thinking, feeling, and acting.

These options can be pursued along four supportive lines:

a. the understanding of one's own motives
b. the recognition of one's values
c. the recognition of one's conceptual framework and of one's understanding of concepts
d. the expression of the significance of thinking, feeling and willing as an atmosphere of being.

The investigation of the Third I then can only result in a feeling of significance, and this capacity to feel must be the capacity of the protreptic guide.

In 1649 the concept of "self-interest" was met for the first time in English. In his "Democracy in America" (1835) Alexis de Tocqueville writes:

> *"[Self-interest] is a doctrine not very lofty, but clear and sure. It does not seek to attain great objects; but it attains those it aims for without too much effort. ... [It] does not produce great devotion; but it suggests little sacrifices each day; by itself it cannot make a man virtuous; but it forms a multitude of citizens who are regulated, temperate, moderate, farsighted, masters of themselves; and if it does not lead directly to virtue through the will, it brings them near to it insensibly through habits."*

The concept of enlightened self-interest has been of enormous economical significance in establishing the picture of the rational agent, entrepreneur, or consumer, but does it actually have any epistemological sense? We can only know these interests by abstracting from ourselves as unique individuals and perceiving ourselves as members of a politically defined group or class, through general anthropological constructions of "man", or as acting "instances" of moral maxims or mores. Perhaps the Natural Law from the seventh century was the first successful attempt at defining a context of minimal self-interest after the Christian dogmas of man in the image of Adam. Jean Jacques Rousseau was a philosopher who a little later fought to alter the picture of man shaped by original sin. His attempts, as an incentive to the republican movements, expressing the overall intellectual aspirations of the enlightenment, and perhaps also the moral influence of pietism, were brought to a preliminary peak in the Declaration of Human Rights. However, the role of human duties seems quickly to be overshadowed by general self-interest in the wake of rapidly growing capitalism. Duty was neglected by neoclassical axioms of the balance of self-interest and information, or absorbed by nationalism and its chauvinism. Not until the raising of the socialist and communist movements was a picture of man trying to balance right and duty beyond enlightened egoism created and this was sadly misused by totalitarianism. But after all, when it comes to personal interests we have to know a lot about ourselves, and it might not be that easy to be enlightened in these matters – as Marx remarked in *Grundrisse* the needs and the content of the propensity to consume are created by the commodities. Thus there is no meta-choice on the market in the sense of a creative choice producing the opportunities which are decided upon. Today this has transformed freedom into a liberalist totalitarianism of the production of consumer identities.

It is not easy, perhaps even impossible, to understand one's own motives from the classical mental models built on instincts, desires, and drives, because it presupposes the understanding of one's self as a character or type – you cannot even identify yourself in this way after hours of watching yourself on camera, not to speak of the construction of this from one's own texts, or from one's works of art; and especially not from description by others. One simply cannot produce one's own caricature. This would imply the objective evaluation of one's own desires, ambitions, prejudices, and emotional bindings, a project which psychoanalysis has attempted in vain by trying to solve the problem through making it possible to approach oneself in the capacity of a child ("as" a child in both senses: being a child, and experiencing this child like a child). The classical cognitive models like the influential ones constructed by Maslow – at the most refined level in his book, "Towards a Psychology of Being"- rationalize existential motivation, elaborating on the y-factor of McGregor, and are able to cast some light on the sense of self-management, but we have to dig deeper. We must also dig deeper than the narrative reconstructions of the self developed by therapists like Michael White in the wake of postmodern criticism of strategically distributed power through the embodiment of a self-controlling and self-suppressive power. The classical analytical approaches are the ones of Michel Foucault and Gilles Deleuze, and their followers like Giorgio Agamben, and the neo-Marxists Paulo Virno, Antonio Negri, Michael Hart and Maurizio Lazaretto – the concept of "bio-politics" being the key concept. (I shall examine the reflective relation to motives further after the passage on rhetoric following).

It is a well kept secret that even an enormous number of stories about your own life will never be able to identify you as a person, not even as a character or as a type. Stories function in another way as self-biographical conjectures, and (this is not meant pejoratively) they transport the weak concept of character or type into a far more dramatic and fantasy-saturated domain. Actually one could claim that stories of the past take place in a virtual or even phantasmagoric future. So, this option must be left out.

The second line along which might lead to self-reflection is the concept of value, but it is complicated due to its ambivalence. Historically we are acquainted with values through commandments, ideals, and virtues. The concept of commandment as an incorporation of values is known primarily from religion. The Ten Commandments are absolute rules of conduct, i.e. of the will, and very often also rules of thought, emotion, and, of course, motives. They correlate with prohibitions. They are indispensable from a Christian point of view and, considered from a functional perspective, they are necessary for upholding a certain state of balance in a society. Thus they have a global, or trans-cultural, character, as a phenomenon.

In the Scholastic tradition Thomas Aquinas distinguishes between "praeceptum" and "mandatum", where "praecepta" are necessary laws of reason without which society is impossible, while "mandata" have a less obligate character, since they contribute to the good, but cannot be stated as commandments or prohibitions. "Praecepta" then operate as absolute principles which must be followed in spite of any inclination to the opposite. They are, as Kant put it, independent of the state of mind of the acting person. In Christian religion, however, the "praecepta" should correlate with positive intentions. The "mandata" on the other hand depend on good will, or even on love ("caritas"), and they demand an ethical fantasy and a propensity to explore the depth of their possible content by acting them out. Ideals have this character and virtues even more so, because a person living through these ideals of values simultaneously has his character shaped (or shapes his character thereby). Thus, they both depend on the capacity of the individual to shape his personality in line with them, "to do the good for the good's own sake", as Aristotle put it in the "Nicomachean Ethics".

Neither ideals nor virtues can be transformed into sheer principles or imperatives, mainly due to the fact that they are by nature too rich in meaning, and too dependent on the uniqueness of the event. Hence, the concept of "core value" means either "ideal" or "virtue". Thus, a person acting on the basis of core values might be said to act "normatively", if these values can be subjects of reflection and deliberation, but they are never 'objective' in the full sense of the word, as far as they can be interpreted with a certain margin, and plainly have to be experienced by being done in order to be understood. Even if learning by being told and by example, are of utter importance to the communication of value, the learning by doing is the main road to their sense. However, values contain principles which cannot be abolished. Considering the five core values of Western culture, the good, the just, the true, the beautiful and their mutual condition, freedom, they allow only to a certain degree for deliberate interpretation. Even the most imperative of all ideals for human interrelations, the golden rule, cannot be realized without relating it to the concrete content of the event and its context. This is easy to see, when we consider that only in relation to a limited set of relations is one able to know what one does not want to be done to oneself. One person might in some situations really want to be seen through, or even exposed, but another might have quite a different inclination in situations seemingly alike or, of course, rather different.

I call the four core values "The Greek Square", because of their origin in Greek philosophy:

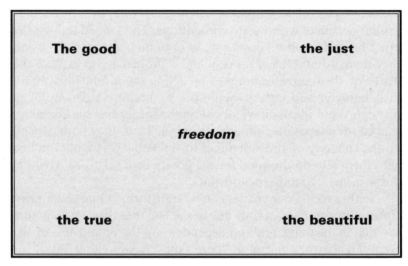

Fig. 3. The Greek Square

The passage to core values might be, if not open straightforward, at least sufficiently realistic to be worth attempting to walk. However, this demands a clarification of our conceptual framework and of our ways with words and the concepts which they contain. Thus also self-understanding goes through analysis of one's own verbal practice. Of course this approach or dive into our inner thesaurus or encyclopedia cannot ignore our personal grammar. This must definitely not be seen as a Lacanian venture, quite the opposite, for what we find is not an unconscious, private language, but the common, social, and historic meaning of words. We confront the sense of sense, and hence, the secrets of communication, because we speak to ourselves all the time as if we were two persons inside ourselves. It is the mode of this dialogue which we have to get a notion of, and especially how we listen to, and hence sanction and

50

accept the course and result of the inner dialogue, a result being cognitive, emotional, or conative.

A way to express the character of this mode is through values, but it can never be pursued until one has come to grips with one's own conceptual practice, i.e. with the way which one uses words as means to the articulation of experienced truth, whether it relates to the mental realm or to the outer world.

Hence, we have to listen to what we actually say to ourselves – because this is what we must do in relation to the other person. "Akroasis" in the Greek, "auscultatio" in the Latin translation, to listen, was a Stoic virtue, alongside its necessary companion, the "prosoché", "attentio", the character and consequences of the individual subjects of attention and their modes.

We all know the phenomenon that we can hear ourselves speaking when we address others and that we can distinguish a certain emotional bent, or tone, tune, color, shade, "value", flavor, brutality or fragrance, authority or exposedness – whatsoever the metaphor – in our own voice giving us a rather seismographic picture of how we actually conceive ourselves in the event and hence, how we conceive the event. We can actually choose to ignore this sound of our own voice and we often forget it, especially when we feel comfortable or safe, or when the words run away with us.

To be able to listen to the sound of this, our very own voice, might be an astonishing and revealing experience as if a door was suddenly opened to a room in which a hidden conversation takes place revealing the frightening factuality of our own speech, even if it is not more than a whisper. The event opens a door to our "inner speakers" and they unite in the voice coming out of our mouth, and which we recognize through the principle of translocutionarity as our way with sense. It is the mode in which our I-1 and I-2 are talking to each other; and whatever the subject, the confrontation is with the way in which I practice sense and sense practices me.

This practice reveals its first trace as the quality of the inner voices which is the "qualitas occultas" of me and the identity of which I so strongly feel as soon as the event shall change their tone and their modulation into what could almost be called an "accent" forced upon my sounding voice by my attempt to speak the foreign tong of the little country of the event.

This phenomenon is very important in protreptic, both as a way in which the protreptic guide becomes consciousness of how he actually feels situated in the dialogue and how he generally experience "being evented", but not the least as a way to prompt the other person to think about himself.

A way to listen to the other person which in the "Topica" of Aristotle is seen as a strategy to oppose the sophistic arguments is "... to refer a term back to its original meaning on the ground that it is more fitting to take it in this sense than in that now established" (II, vi, 34).

However, we cannot accept the criterion of "fitting" without examining it further. If etymology should be a reliable method, and I think it has much power to it, the travel back into the semantics of words should fasten them to the relation between the body and the world. This could certainly prevent the shallow play with words performed by the sophists, but it must also make us wiser about life and about ourselves.

Let us take a simple example: the word "wise", Old English *wis,* from Proto Germanic **wisaz* (compare "wizard"), comes from the Proto Indo-European base **woid-/*weid-/*wid-* "to see," hence "to know".

It is important to consider that "wise" means knowing from the act of having seen, not from the act of being told. No one can teach you to be wise, you must accomplish it yourself. Hence, you have a statement of wisdom which could mean something to your own practice.

On the whole the analysis of the diairetic[18] sense, and not at least the etymology of words, are very important protreptic instruments. This analytic strategy is developed by classical Greek dialectics, and the thinker of our time who revived it and explored its depths was Martin Heidegger, whose opus was pervaded totally by this retrieval of the historical roots of words as an epistemological and ontological approach.

---

18 In Plato's philosophy "diairesis" means the conceptual analyses of the relation between genus and species of a word: Mammal, man, Chinese, Danish ... etc. It is obvious that the logic/semantic relations will depend on the criterion chosen. Mammal, man, language-using, technology-using, culture-developing. Or Mammal, man, woman, educated woman. Etc.

The word "dream" could serve as another example of this procedure. In a protreptic dialogue this could easily be a word the protreptic guide seeks the meaning of. Answers shall soon reveal the analytic distinctions within the word between the states of being awake or sleeping, and between vision and utopia, on the one side, and illusion and phantasm on the other. Qualities like "pleasant" and "terrible" could be supplemented, as could "realistic" and "unreal". Dreaming could also be related to hoping and planning, to strategy and chance, just like the distinction between individual and collective visions are important. In particular, the practice of collective dream-building distinguishes leadership as a means of embodying sense in the organization and people have stated that we live in a "dream society", positively related to the so called "experience economy", even if a few might sense that it is a nightmare gathering.

But a travel into the etymology of dreaming is also able to reveal something about the possible sense which the word might have for our personal use of it. According to "The Online Etymological Dictionary", Douglas Harper (which is most often used in this book when issues are about English etymology) the word is first met in 1250 in the sense "sequence of sensations passing through a sleeping person's mind," probably related to O.N. *draumr*, Dan. *drøm*, Swed. *drom*, O.S. *drom*, Du. *droom*, O.H.G. *troum*, Ger. *traum* "dream," perhaps from W.Gmc. **draugmas* "deception, illusion, phantasm" (cf. O.S. *bidriogan*, O.H.G. *triogan*, Ger. *trügen* "to deceive, delude," O.N. *draugr* "ghost, apparition"). Possible cognates outside Gmc. are Skt. *druh-* "seek to harm, injure," Avestan *druz-* "lie, deceive." But O.E. *dream* meant only "joy, mirth," also "music." Words for "sleeping vision" in O.E. were *mæting* and *swefn* (from PIE **swep-no-,* cf. Gk. *hypnos*). Much study has failed to prove that O.E. *dream* "noisy merriment" is the root of the modern word for "sleeping vision," despite being identical in spelling. Either the meaning of the word changed dramatically or "vision" was an unrecorded secondary O.E. meaning of *dream*, or there are two separate words here. "It seems as if the presence of *dream* 'joy, mirth, music,' had caused *dream* "illusion", to be avoided, at least in literature, and *swefn,* lit. 'sleep,' to be substituted" [OED]. *Dream* in the sense of "ideal or aspiration" is from 1931, from the earlier sense of "something of dream-like beauty or charm" (1888). *Dreamy* is from 1567 in the sense "full of dreams;" from 1941 originates its sense as "perfect, ideal." *Dreamboat* a "romantically desirable person" is from 1947. *Dreamland* is c.1834; *dreamscape* is 1959, in a Sylvia Plath poem."

It is significant that dreaming relates not only to deceiving and lying, but also to seeking to harm or injure, and that its original sense in Old English seems to have been "joy, mirth, or music". Hence, the threatening and destructive aspects of dreaming, and even the dimension of knowledge (of self, past, and future) so important in antique oneirology as the hermeneutic of sleeping visions, were left out on behalf of the euphoric aspect. In modern branding as a function of what Rolf Jensen called "Dream Society", this Old English sense seems to have taken over again, but the dark sides of dreaming are lying just beneath the glittering surface of spectacular promises of eternal happiness. From such considerations the way in which a manager uses dreams could be clarified as a means to acquire an increased consciousness of one's own attitude to the organizational tasks—both the euphoric and the dark aspects.

The therapies of Freud and Jung were intensely focused on dreaming as part of an internal 'language' of a personal or transpersonal grammar and semantic. A dream is generally structured around events and voices. It would be almost too obvious to hypothesize that in dreams the two separate "I's" are embodied in dramatic characters, and that the "Third I" is represented in the mood or atmosphere of the dream. This was, understandably enough, the approach of ancient oneirology presupposing that voices might be incorporations of transcendent and omniscient powers and that events might be omens of things to happen with moods the signs of their outcome. Anyhow, whatever the interpretational framework, it must be conceded that dreams are important parts of our mental life and cannot be ignored as expressions of the fate of values in our lives.

Take the frequent dream among many people that you have slain a person and hidden the body somewhere and that you fear to de discovered. The hermeneutics of this dream might relate to recent events, or to the clasp of inner forces, or whatever. But the fact of the dream lies in its mood, the despairing sense of guilt. This mood is the "message" of the dream. Perhaps it is nothing but an inner expression of this state as a basic and virtual state of being and nothing more? Why relate it hermeneutically to childhood experiences, Oedipus-complexes and the like. It is just an existential mood presented to us as a way of being.

Then the importance yielded to it by the protreptic guide must be its possibility of letting us explore this mood, and to estimate its role in our lives – not its function, since symptomatic interpretations are always just hypotheses or even postulates.

Protreptic, however, would not use dreams as a part of its method if it is done before an audience, unless the other person insists or the event of dialogue strongly suggests it. In front of an audience dreams would seldom be part of the dialogue due to the level of individual intimacy implicated by them.

The use of protreptic in the organization with the employees as an audience is of course my invention. During antiquity, conversations before an audience between philosophers and sophist were very common, but these were emulations, competitions about the power of arguing which protreptic can never be.

Protrepic done between two persons alone in a room is its classical form. But protreptic done with groups of employees at the same or at different levels is of course also a possibility. What is problematic is whether a leader can serve as a protreptic guide and, if granted, then how? Alternatives could be the employees doing it themselves, or having a "professional" protreptic guide facilitating the process. Answers here are dependent on context, culture and attitudes, but also of the kind of problems faced.

8.

The guiding images of the protreptic dialogue

The basic attitude of the protreptic speaker is *earnestness* and *seriousness.*

"Earnest" origins in O.E. "eornoste" (adj.) from a noun "eornost", "passion, zeal" (surviving only in the phrase in earnest), from P.Gmc. *ern "vigor, briskness" (cf. O.H.G. "arnust" "struggle," Goth. "arniba" "safely," O.N. jarna "fight, combat") The proper name Ernest (lit. "resolute") is from the same root.

These etymological roots reveal the content of passion, zealousness, and the struggle with oneself, which a permanent attitude of seriousness or earnestness demands, and where the winner is the Self. The outcome of this victory would always manifest itself as a harmonization of thought, emotion, and will. One has become able to will one's will. Earnestness must then be seen as the courage to shape the event in a normative direction. This does not imply that such norms cannot be intertwined in power and negative intentions, but in many situations it demands courage to break through the general shallowness, smartness, and indifference of attitudes (the protreptic guide must of course know that he himself is also prone to these attitudes, and must remove the beam in his own I before attending to the mote in the other person's).

"Serious" can be traced back to 1440, "expressing earnest purpose or thought" (of persons), from M.Fr. "sérieux", "grave, earnest" (14c.), from L. "seriosus", from L. "serius" "weighty, important, grave," probably from a PIE base *swer- (cf. Lith. sveriu "to weigh, lift," svarus" "heavy;" O.E. "swære" "heavy," Ger. "schwer" "heavy," Goth. "swers" "honored, esteemed," lit. "weighty"). As opposite of jesting, from 1712; as opposite of light (of music, theater, etc.), from 1762. Meaning "attended with danger" is from 1800. The phrase to take (something) seriously is attested from

1782. This metaphorical basis of a weight is preserved in the concept "gravity", from "gravitas", heavy, in Latin, traceable to 1541, from M.Fr. grave, from L. "gravis" "weighty, serious, heavy," from PIE base *gru- (cf. Skt. guruh "heavy, weighty;" Gk. "baros", "weight," barys "heavy;" Goth. "kaurus" "heavy").

There might be some differences in significance between earnest, serious, and grave. One can speak in earnest, which means, that it is possible not to do so, i.e. to feign the state of mind. Of course seriousness can also be simulated, but "serious" has far more figurative senses, like serious illness, serious attempt, serious artist, serious objections, obstacles, and chances. These senses point to the fact that earnestness is bound to an intentional state of mind, since the adjective "earnest" would hardly be able to substitute "serious". One could say that earnest has perhaps a slightly deeper existential sense than serious, even if serious also has this relation to the truth of articulated intentions and intentional states of mind; but seriousness might be more strategic, even threatening, ("You should take this very seriously my friend!") a connotation not that obvious in earnestness.

"Grave" on the other hand can replace serious in many cases, but has its own significance by denoting the solemn, ceremonious, and the somber or gloomy, the dignified, and the distressing and even tragic. Probably earnest is the most spontaneous or naturally expressive of the words, while grave signifies the ritual, ceremonial, and socially codified manifestation of certain emotions connected to sorrow.

The concept of earnestness must then be chosen to denote the attitude of the protreptic, also while it has a certain light flavor, and the least deliberate ring to it. It was philosophically explored by Soeren Kierkegaard as an individual's authentic attitude towards his own being. In his book "Begrebet Angest" ("The Concept of Angst") he states that earnestness is related to living, not to speculative philosophy. It is the sense of man as the synthesis of the finite and the infinite; and in the effort of earnestness one has to turn towards one's own being and not to lose oneself in the interest of external objects and doings. To be real means to turn to one's own soul and to God. Here, as in his emphasis on the positive relation of humor and earnestness, Kierkegaard owes much to Plato, which is explicitly articulated by his opus in the admiration of Socrates – his doctoral thesis from 1841 is a study of Socrates' irony: *Om Begrebet* Ironi. *Med stadigt Hensyn til Socrates*. 1841. ("About the Concept of Irony. Permanently Considering Socrates").[19]

In philosophy, Plato is the first really to emphasize earnestness, "spoudé", as a core ethical attitude. Thus it is often used synonymously with the intention of the good ("aréte") person (Resp. 423 d; 603 c; Leg. 757, a; 814 e.). Plato distinguished hierarchically between three different objects of earnestness in human matters, presupposing that God comes before anything else: one's own soul, one's body, and one's property (Leg. 743 e).

It is characteristic of Plato's way of thinking that he does not place earnestness in opposition to play and to jest, fun, and joke, even if he would not allow a role for it in comedy. In his sixth letter he claims that earnestness and play are brothers ("adelphe"); but this presupposes a concept of serious play and humor. Aristotle does not contribute anything further to this subject.

In relation to protreptic it is important that the earnestness of the protreptic guide is mild, and that the hard labor of self reflection sometimes can be seen in the mirror of humor. Earnest self irony is also an acceptable way in which to establish symmetry on the side of the protreptic guide. By the way: the dual nature of the word is played upon virtuously in Oscar Wilde's "The Importance of Being Earnest".

It is of immense importance that the protreptic guide does not manipulate in any way. Simulation and acting are not the only ways of manipulation, but they are always tempting. As Aristotle says in the first chapter of Book III of his "Art of rhetoric" such devices must if possible be avoided. However the role of style ("lexis"), delivery of speech, ("dynamis") and acting ("hypókrisis"), must not be underrated in order to be persuasive and convincing – the Greek language does not differentiate between to persuade and to convince; they are both called "peithein". However there is a great difference between persuading and convincing. Even if they both might happen against the knowledge of the one being addressed,

---

19 In 1954 the German philosopher, Michael Theunissen wrote his important doctoral thesis, *Der Begriff Ernst bei Søren Kierkegaard.*

convincing is far more often understood as a process, which does not manipulate the will and the emotions of the other person, in contrast to persuasion.

The style of the protreptic guide must then be spontaneously kind, sober, and based on argument. However, the goal of the protreptic guide is to confront the other person with himself, and the dialogue must be controlled by the guide, not through inquisition, but through the presentation of options. Often he must state what he thinks and feels himself, before he challenges the other person to do the same. This is the proper meaning of earnestness. The guide must invest himself in the speech, and he must not fear exposition.

These attitudes could be expressed by three basic phenomena, which dominate the protreptic dialogue, often of a genuine symbolic nature, or genuine metaphors, but also more than metaphors: the mirror, the face, and the voice.

The mirror

The protreptic mirror on the one hand shows a picture of the one, who we are, even if it must be necessarily blurred, and must have a bias of ambiguity borne by the perception of the protreptic and by the event. On the other hand it presents us with a picture of the one, who we might be, if we really turn to our basic values, opening a virtual, nameless anonymity. It is a creative mirroring. In order to realize this mirroring of a potential becoming, the one who does the mirroring must himself appear as a human being.

In the dialogue "Alcibiades", probably the most authentic of the disputed dialogues, Plato writes about the eye as a mirror in 123D:

SOCRATES: Consider in your turn: suppose that, instead of speaking to a man, it said to the eye of one of us, as a piece of advice "See thyself," how should we apprehend the meaning of the admonition? Would it not be, that the eye should look at that by looking at which it would see itself?

ALCIBIADES: Clearly.

SOCRATES: Then let us think what object there is anywhere, by looking at which [132e] we can see both it and ourselves.

ALCIBIADES: Why, clearly, Socrates, mirrors and things of that sort.

SOCRATES: Quite right. And there is also something of that sort in the eye that we see with?

ALCIBIADES: To be sure.

SOCRATES: And have you observed that the face of the person who looks into another's eye is shown in the optic confronting him, [133a] as in a mirror, and we call this the pupil ("koré"), for in a sort of way it is an image of the person looking?

[133b] ALCIBIADES: That is true.

SOCRATES: Then an eye viewing another eye, and looking at the most perfect part of it, the thing wherewith it sees, will thus see itself.

ALCIBIADES: Apparently.

SOCRATES: But if it looks at any other thing in man or at anything in nature but what resembles this, it will not see itself.

ALCIBIADES: That is true.

SOCRATES: Then if an eye is to see itself, it must look at an eye, and at that region of the eye in which the virtue of an eye is found to occur; and this, I presume, is sight.

ALCIBIADES: That is so.

SOCRATES: And if the soul too, my dear Alcibiades, is to know herself, she must surely look at a soul, and especially at that region of it in which occurs the virtue of a soul – wisdom, and at any other part of a soul which resembles this?

ALCIBIADES: I agree, Socrates.

So, the soul of the protreptic guide, and its wisdom, must be the mirror for the other person.

Soon after Nero's accession in 54 CE, his tutor, the philosopher Seneca, addressed his young pupil with an essay called *De Clementia* in which he offered advice on how to behave in his new role. This is an exhortatory address to Nero, and it advocates mercy as the sovereign quality for a Roman emperor. The first lines go:

"To write on clemency, Oh, Emperor Hero, I have decided ("institutui"), in order to be in a way a of mirror ("specu-

*lum"), and to show you to yourself as a human being, who
could become the greatest pleasure to all people."*

It is certainly with deliberation that Seneca chooses the verb "in-
stitui", because it reinforces the content of the mirror. "Institutui" both means to "decide", to "institute", and to "teach", but it
also means to "plant" a tree or a sprout (to do the good). Seneca
does not only say "I offer to be a mirror for you, great Emperor".
In the unsaid he also 'says' "In the silence of the mirror, visible
through the spaces between the letters, I dare to challenge your
power through a power far greater than yours, coming from a place
where all power is annihilated."

In 64 A.D. Nero had had enough of this mirror and Seneca
was forced to take his own life.

It is very often seen how a mother imitate her child's facial
expressions in order to signal that she understands its needs. Imita-
tion developed by analogy from this prototypical situation is foreign to protreptic, though performed by some therapeutic schools.
But the protreptic guide also repeats by interpreting the value basis
expressed by the other person. He forces him gently to stick to his
words.

The face

The only early place in Western philosophy in which the human
face plays a certain role is in the philosophy of Plotinus and the
Neo-Platonists. It is not until the great metaphysical synthesis by
the Kabbalist Isaac Luria from Safed, in the sixteenth century
(1534-1572), that the face really becomes important. Western Christian philosophy did not have its prohibition against images realized
until the reformation, and was never followed, of course, by the
Orthodox Russian Church with its iconography.

However, in Muslim Sufism we encounter a perhaps Plotinian-
inspired emphasis on the human face, by Isaac Luria called "shek-
hina", the light of God potentially incorporated in any human
being, a tradition incorporated in Hassidic Judaism. The Christian concept of "plesion", our "neighbor" also could have this
connotation.

Kamuran Godelek writes in his article on *Sufi Philosophy The Neoplatonist Roots of Sufi Philosophy*:[20]

"Sufism assumes that there is a union of God, universe and humans, and that human beings are an appearance of God; but God's appearance in the shape of a human being cannot be thought of any further than just an appearance. The reality is not a duality between God and humans, but rather a sameness, oneness between them. A person is a talking, thinking, acting God… It is possible that the belief of oneness of humans and God in Sufism is carried over from Neoplatonism. In the trilogy of God-Universe-Humans, God has the highest position, second is the universe, and third are human beings. Even though humans rank last in the trilogy, they are very close to the God, and almost identical to him because of the soul they have.

Sufism and Neoplatonism share the same beliefs about the soul. According to Neoplatonism, the soul is a divine essence, a substance, the source of all existence. The soul is the effect, image, or copy of pure thought, namely God…

For Neoplatonism beauty means much more than mere symmetry. It involves a close relationship to the ideal reality; it is an appearance of God over the objects of the universe. Whatever the divine light shines on becomes beautiful. Sufism thinks exactly the same about beauty. In Sufism, beauty is expressed with "cemal" meaning human face, the beauty of human face. What is really expressed in "cemal" (human face) is the appearance of divine light in the face of a human. Neoplatonism identified beauty with divine essence, and sufism adopted the same idea. This is beautifully expressed in the following verse from Husrev:

Want to understand an example of the real essence of God?

Look at the face of a beautiful woman and there see the face of God.

Realizing divine characteristics in human beauty might be an influence of Neoplatonism in Sufi philosophy."

---

20 *www.muslimphilosophy.com/ip/CompGode.htm - 22k -*

In the twentieth century philosophy Jewish thinkers such as Martin Buber and Emmanuel Lévinas carried on the Hassidic tradition in creating a new conceptual framework of the problem of other minds. In their opinion every face was sacred and could not, and ought not, to be transformed into an object.

From their perspective dialogue must emerge from the face of the other person, because it insists in its absolute being, which means its irreducibility, and with a character beyond the object. It summons in its silence and inviolability. Lévinas in his book "Totality and Infinity" talks about the issue that the "origin of language lays in the face", and that "the first meaning of all speech is the face". The face, however, must not be understood as something which we are able to experience spontaneously through looking at it. It signifies more, like our own face, that which, through the enigma in the mirror, can never belong fully to us. The epiphany of the face through language communicates the demand of the ethical inviolability of the other person by the very fact that we are able to wound it. Remember that executions by shooting are normally effectuated through the neck, and that people facing the executioners get a black cloth over their eyes, probably because the soldiers cannot bear to see that they are seen. From this perspective Lévinas also seems to operate with a sense of significance in relation to the face of the other person, because the face is a basic event. The face appearing in dialogue as an event of the event is transcendent, and must be kept in its fundamental anonymity, because it is the face of all faces, or anybody's face, the "shekhinah". Any interpretation makes the awe-inspiring factuality of the face disappear. The face resists being read, it defends an impenetrable autonomy.

However, this way of experiencing is not natural. It demands a great, great effort in every event. When Lévinas exemplifies it with the relation of the teacher and pupil he breaks with his own premises, because this relation is built on another, specific authority, investing role-power in the face of the teacher, not anonymity. Of course his thought ought to be scrutinized from socio-economical contexts, which would point at the fact that either we speak about a very small and closed society, or a mass society, and that in neither of these types can the ideal be realized. But perhaps it could be approached in the protreptic dialogue; certainly the ideal is beautiful.

The voice

The Greek-Jewish philosopher, Philon af Alexandria (death 40 A.D.) writes about the decalogue that God never spoke with a real voice, but that his words were emanations of light, like our own inner light. The eye of the soul, which projects this light, is able to grasp the light of God as sense, because our own voice is itself made by light. This opens to another kind of insight. He shows us that the essence of voice is light, and that its bottom is darkness. The insight hiding here is the simple one that what unites the voice and silence, is death.

If we really dare look at the face of the other person and to listen to him, it always shows us the unique connection between voice and silence, revealing the identity of a human being by pointing to the existence of its Third I. As Plato said, the body is the tomb of the soul, and the face is a sepulchral monument, a silent inscription despite its possible vivacity, a vivacity the animating power of which can die any second. The proteptic guide must neither fear this inner silence, in himself or in others, nor the impending death away from the event – which is not a physical death in the proper sense, but a turning back into the infinite cavity of the Third I. The protreptic guide must be worthy of this silence, and of this death, by carrying it out as his own silence.

Silence is a kind of nakedness, accepting the glance of the other, and not resisting interpretation and its inherent misrepresentation or even distortion. Though, at the same time silence is a mixture of both spontaneous and reflective chastity – the Greeks made "chastity" into a goddess, "Aidos", in front of whom anybody had to cast down his eyes in awe. That is why the face is sacred or holy – the latter in Old Nordic meaning "godlike". Silence can be seen too as a way to lower the voice before the presence of the other person, and this attitude must be the one of the protreptic guide.

This is where protreptic must begin, at the silence of and the death inside the other person. This is why the attitude of the protreptic guide is earnestness. However, this silence might both be desperate and happy. The protreptic guide must know both these aspects of the silence of the death of mind. He must be able to feel it in his own face. But the form which death embodies in the face which is speaking and watching is the soft and mild silence of my own voice.

The voice of the other person is always a manifestation of his own inner dialogue between I-1 and I-2, and of the presence of his Third I. In relation to other people deception is the natural state, meaning "not to be completely honest". However, this mode is projected into the dialogue of the mind, and most people betray themselves at some level sometimes. But this does not mean that there should be a truth. Truth must be produced.

Silence originates in the individual, but it could be shared. That is why the words are able to shine in the intense conversations, as the effort to speak and listen as carefully as we possibly can create a zone of light between us. The face is always enlightened from the center of the dialogue protruding from the darkness of the event and its context into a greater light, like a Claire-obscure.

The person whose face cannot light up, cannot listen, and the one who cannot listen, cannot talk properly. The protreptic guide must keep the power over the event while at the same time honoring it. He must be able to survey it, to foresee its course, and lead it towards mutual insight, and to receive its gifts and hazards. Thus the protreptic guide has to expect that he too will learn something from the conversation.

The light in the dialogue gives it transparence and perspicuity ("safés" in Stoic philosophy). It must never "be mean, nor above the dignity of the subject." (Rhe. III, ii, 2). The dialogue is led for the sake of the other person, but it must neither be reproaching nor instructing. If moral issues pop up which are contrary to the guide's, and perhaps intolerable, like racism, the dialogue must either be brought to an end, or the guide must lead the other person to contradict himself, and through this realize that he was wrong. The best would be to search for the essence of his attitudes, and together explore what they really mean. To a racist one could ask the question: "If a colored person is going to save your life, would you accept it?" Probably most people would say "yes", and one could then ask "What is it that you expect colored persons could do to you which you would not accept?"

This would very likely be the same as that which he would not accept from white people. But if he then states that he would accept insults from white people which he would not accept from black people, one can ask him why. If he answers, that black people are less careful, one can ask for examples. If he is able to give some, one can ask whether white people could not act in the same way. If he then states that he has never experienced such things with white people, one can ask, whether he thinks that bad white people do not exist. He might then answer that they are a minority, and one can once more ask him why. Again, his answer could be that this is due to race. It is easy here to give counter examples of bad white people, and at the same time show that they act badly due to circumstances – oppression, desperation, hate, stupidity; after all Hitler and the Nazis were white. He can then claim that Mao was yellow. From such examples it is again easy to show that people are bad because they want power, and that the black persons have very little power. And so on. In the end he will not be able to prove that black people are more bad than white.

This fragment of a dialogue points to the content of the pro-treptic dialogue. Let us look at some ideal or typical courses which this dialogue may take.

9.

The content of the protreptic dialogue

What is then the content of the protreptic dialogue? It consists at least of some of the following elements, if we construct a scenario with a protreptic guide and a leader as the one who answers:

1. The protreptic guide asks about the meaning of a word denoting a value:
   Protreptic guide: "What is responsibility?"
   The art is here what Horace in his Ars Poetica, 46, named "callida juncture", "the trick of the connection", to make old words seem new, since most people have become too used to most words to really think about them; and thus the value referred to is blurred.
2. The answers given by the addressed consist of
   Propositions about the values, criteria, and motives as they appear to him in the capacity of true expressions of his inner states of mind:
   The addressed: "I think that any person has to be responsible".
3. Propositions about the false and genuine sense of the words which cover the concepts:
   The protreptic guide asks: "Whom do you have to be responsible to as a leader?"
   The addressed: "Towards the stakeholders, and especially towards my superior and towards the employees. Not towards people in other firms. Or, I should think that there are several senses of responsibility implying different obligations."
4. Propositions about his past acts and the inherent relations between these acts, whether in the form of knowledge about how events and their contextual settings influenced these acts, or in proper narratives:
   The protreptic guide: "So you feel urged to be responsible? You spoke about obligations?"

The addressed: "I was brought up this way!" "My story is about a man who always wanted to anticipate what is expected from him".

5. Propositions about moods and hence, about significance of ways of being in events.
   The protreptic guide: "So it gives you satisfaction to accept this obligation? What do you feel?"
   The adressed: "It depends. Sometimes it is too much. It overwhelms me and blocks my capacity to be a consequential leader."

6. Propositions about the consequences, which his values have for his relations to other people:
   The protreptic guide: "What do you do then?"
   The addressed: "I try to look at people as employees, not as human beings. But it gives me worries."

7. Propositions about the implications of the values for his relation to himself:
   The protreptic guide: "And what do these worries tell you?"
   The addressed: "That it is hard for me to be obliged to treat people as I did not want to be treated myself."

It is obvious that these propositions are dialectical in the sense that Aristotle used in his "Topica", which means that they can never refer to an apodictic basis, but must seek the "endoxa", the set of intelligent common-sense opinions as their point of orientation. Thus the protreptic dialogue can never aspire to create an axiological reduction in the sense that the participant should be able to reach any absolute certainty.[21]

---

21 Hence, what the German philosopher Leonard Nelson named "regressive abstraction" as a means to pursue the original judgments in his attempt to re-actualize Socratic dialogue, can never obtain apodictic certainty – which, of course, must be his opinion too, being a follower of the Friesian School: "By analysing conceded judgements we go back to their presuppositions. We operate regressively from the consequences to the reason. In this regression, we eliminate the accidental fact to which the particular judgement relates and by this separation bring into relief the original assumption that lies at the bottom of the judgement on the concrete instance." (Quoted from , *Die sokratische Methode*, by Leonard Nelson, translated by Thomas K. Brown III. Internet: *www.friesian.com/method.htm*).

The famous definition of reasoning in the beginning of the "Topica" (I, 100a, 23), goes as follows:

"Reasoning (syllogismòs) is a discussion (logos) in which, certain things having been laid down, something other than these things necessarily results through them. Reasoning is demonstrative (apódeizis) when it proceeds from premises which are true and primary or of such a kind that we have derived our original knowledge of them through premises which are primary and true. Reasoning is dialectical which reasons from generally accepted opinions (hó ex endoxon syllogizómenos')."

By "discussion" (logos) must, of course, both mean the inner dialogue in the sense of Plato, as well as the dialogue with another person (the Stoic distinction between "logos endiathetos" and "logos prophoricos", the internal and external voice).

Aristotle here seems to favor a sort of consensus-theory of knowledge which seems obviously tilted towards the social objectivity of self-reflection:

"The number of ways in which the propositions must be selected is the same as the number of distinctions which we have made regarding propositions. One may choose either universal opinions (pánton doxas), or those of the majority, or those of the wise – or all of them, or of the majority of the most famous – or opinions contrary to those generally held, and also opinions which are in accord with the arts." (Topica, I, xiv, 35, 105a-105b).

The pragmatism of a man feeling obliged towards the "paideia" of the polis, and recognizing his debt to tradition, is strongly experienced, and even foreign to our inclination towards individualism. However, it must of course be the *conditio sine qua non* for any dialogue that values and forms of thought are shared. The point of departure between him and us in relation to the expert or elite culture advocated by Aristotle, perhaps especially in the matter of ethics, is set by the modern power of democracy. The difference is, however, not overwhelming:

"Furthermore, you must define what kinds of things should be called as the majority call them, and what should not; for this is useful both for constructive and destructive purposes ("kataskeuazein" and "anaskeuazein"). For instance, you ought to lay it down that things ought to be described in the language used by the majority, but when it is asked what things are of certain kinds and what are not, you must no longer pay attention to the majority. For example, you must say, as does the majority, that "healthy" is that which is productive of health; but when it is asked whether the subject under discussion is productive of health or not, you must no longer use the language of the majority, but that of the doctor." (Topica, II, ii, 15-20, 110a).

These predicaments concerning the relation between expert vocabulary and common sense language are pertinent to protreptic when the task is to distinguish it from therapy and coaching. The problem is whether there exists a scientific vocabulary of the mind or not. All investigations of the mind which are not exclusively limited to biology or neurology must rest on introspection, also psychology – and also genetic research "just" combines common place concepts of human properties or qualities with scientific propositions about allocations in the brain. Since introspection is led through common sense and its language games, the hyper-meta-vocabulary of the mind is the "endoxa", the intelligent "doxa", the enlightened common sense. This is the core assumption of the "Topica". Hence, Aristotle can develop his protreptic method primarily through the analysis of the syllogism, the dynamic grammar of language games, i.e. through the analysis of the relation between universals and particulars, as they appear in the complicated relation between the elements of propositions and the problems built on them, between definition, property, genus and accident (hóros, idion, génos, and symbebekós). The method is the Platonic "diairesis" (the analytical process moving from the singular object through the species and the differentia to the genus, and back again) and its destructive (anaskeuastikà) and constructive (kataskeuastikà) procedures. But this practice presupposes a very meticulous knowledge of the sense of words, and their inherent absolute or contextual ambiguity (homonoma/homonyma), with which he deals in the Topica from Book I, xv, and onwards. This is not in the least justified by the fact that Sophist arguments usually explore the possibilities of equivocation with manipulative and – from the perspective on philosophy as a practice of liberation – malicious intent.

10.

The ethics of protreptic

Protreptic is a practice of questioning. It consists in asking questions to oneself and to the other person(s). However, it must not carry any trace of an interrogation or examination, and as an enquiry it must be a mutual effort.

The questions are about the sense of the words representing values, and they neither aim at confessions from the other as to his sincerity in living values, nor do they ever doubt his honesty directly. The questioned must do this himself. By his questioning, the protreptic guide searches for possible paradoxes between levels of values in the mind of the other. The aim is never to expose the other to anyone but to himself, since the basic attitude of the protreptic guide is protective.

It would be wrong to say that the protreptic guide wants to cure the other person, because he has no right to distinguish between ill and healthy, but he will assist the other in realizing whether he needs, and wants, to take care of himself. However, this is not done normatively by projecting a model of healthiness of mind, or of mental balance, but only by pointing at inconsistencies in what the other person says about the sense of words, values, and his own thought and emotions. This means that the protreptic guide must operate with an ad hoc hypothesis of a possible mental balance in the other which must of course rely on a more general model of such a balance between passion, thought and will. This mode, however, is not naturalistic, it must be developed by the addressed himself.

Thus, protreptic finds itself alienated by any approach presupposing a "symptomatology".

From this perspective protreptic only shares some traits with therapy, in particular the intention to assist in personal liberations from unwanted opinions, thoughts, projections, and passions, and from experiences and images of oneself which are felt as forced and not chosen.

By always beginning by questioning, the protreptic method signals the Socratic "maieutics", and the more general "peirastic" procedures too, but it would never underwrite the dark side of dialectic, its eristic or agonistic part as described by Aristotle in his "On Sophistical Refutations". Protreptic plainly refuses to understand the rationality of defeating a dialogical opponent, because in protreptic conversations people are not opponents, but partners.

When Aristotle talks about one way to defeat a sophist, "An elementary rule for obtaining a fallacious or paradoxical statement is not to put any thesis directly but to pretend that one is asking from a desire to learn; for this method of inquiry gives an opening for attack." (Soph. elen. XII, 23-25, 172b), he is not following the way of protreptic. The reason for mentioning this at all is that the protreptic dialogue, at least in the beginning, could be misunderstood in this way, i.e. as a manipulative project of rhetoric.

However, it must be beyond doubt that the protreptic guide ought to ask as if he did not know the answer – for example about what "recognition" is, or could be understood as – but this is due to the fact that he must try to learn something, if he shall succeed in making the dialogue intense enough. In this he is very much like the master musician, who does not play his solos for the sake of performance alone, but in order to explore what he actually is able to do by doing it. The latter can only be obtained through the help of the audience. It is easy enough to learn from one's own way of asking, and of course from the way the other person answers, because no two people would answer the same question identically. Our mind's rooms do not have the same arrangement of furniture.

The above quoted sentence from Aristotle is followed almost immediately by another, which is of great importance to the method of protreptic. This is why it is quoted in its considerable length.

"Furthermore you should seek for paradoxes in men's wishes and professed opinions. For they do not wish the same things as they declare that they wish, but they give utterance to the most becoming sentiments, whereas they desire what they think is to their interest. They declare, for example, that a noble death ought to be preferred to a pleasurable life and honorable poverty to discreditable wealth; but their wishes are the opposite of their

words. He, therefore, whose statements agree with his wishes must be led to express the opinions usually professed, and he whose statements agree with the latter must be led to state the opinions usually hidden; for in both cases they must necessarily fall into paradox, for they will contradict either their professed or their secret opinions." (Soph. elen. XII, 36ff, 173a)

In protreptic this unveiling need not be unpleasant, because it can only be done through the help of the other person himself. The common sense ("koiné aisthesis" or "doxa") is the subject of critique on behalf of protreptic, so the goal is quite different. It is not to unmask the other person, but the ideas and opinions which everybody seems to hold, and the way they are usually expressed. The personal unmasking hinted at by Aristotle cannot be done by the protreptic guide; this would be an encroachment, and would always rest on hypothesis, on an all too candid intimacy on the other's behalf. The protreptic guide might share the passion of the detective, but the only crime which he can find is the one which the other person has done to himself. However, the protreptic is not an itinerant exhibiter of the Ibsenian "life-lie"; on the contrary he is the guardian of lives, also of the ones apparently based on mendacity.

So, if somebody states opinions which seem to agree with his wishes, he must be asked what he thinks he really wants, because this might exactly be dictated by common sense. Then there is no paradox, even if he proves himself ashamed of saying that he prefers a pleasurable life from an honorable death, because the point of protreptic is that he might not know what is meant by either of these terms. The person, whose opinions agree with common sense, could be challenged as Aristotle wishes, as to the secret opinions, but these opinions belong to the common sense conception as a shadow. Hence, they are not personal, and ought not to be exposed as individual, moral faults.

In his *Art of Rhetoric* Aristotle talks about the above quoted search for paradox in the opponent's opinions, that "This topic is the most weighty of those that deal with paradox." (II, xxiii,16). Thus he must conceive of this technique of questioning as rhetoric.

11.

The method of protreptic

The method of protreptic is built on dialectics. The central logical form of argument is the enthymeme, a syllogism used by rhetoric as its trade mark.

> *"There are two kinds of enthymemes, the one demonstrative (deiktika), which proves that a thing is or is not, and the other refutative (elenktika), the two differing like refutation and syllogism in Dialectic. The demonstrative syllogism (deiktikon enthúmema) draws conclusions from admitted premises (homologouménon), the refutative draws conclusions disputed (anomoloúgomena) by the adversary." (Rhe. II, xxii, 14-16)*

Thus dialectical argument is developed through "demonstrative" and "refutative" enthymemes which are syllogisms, and "apparent enthymemes, which are not really enthymemes, since they are not syllogisms." (Rhe. II, xxii, 17).

The point of departure is always hypothetical or regulative, since it is oriented towards a knowledge of the definition of a concept, which covers a complex of values, and hence, a knowledge of the essence of these values. This knowledge can never be based on absolute certainty, since values can neither be defined through knowledge of their necessary and sufficient conditions, nor through an a priori knowledge of their essence.

A leading principle is the distinction between ethical, physical and logical propositions, which Aristotle makes in the "Topica" I, xiv. In particular, ethical propositions cannot be treated through a principle of absolute truth:

> *"For philosophical purposes we must deal with propositions from the point of view of truth, but for purposes of dialectic, with a view to opinion ("doxa"). Propositions must always be taken in*

> *their most universal form, and the one should be made into many;*
> *for example, "The knowledge of opposites ("antikeiménon") is*
> *the same," then "The knowledge of contraries ("enantíon") is*
> *the same", and finally "The knowledge of relative terms is the*
> *same." In the same way, those too must be divided again, as long*
> *as division is possible, for example, "the knowledge of good and*
> *evil", "of black and white", and "of cold and hot is the same";*
> *and so with the other cases." (Topica, I, xiv, 30ff)*

This is the principle of the diairetic method of Plato. It is closely related to an analysis of the sense and significance of the concepts used, and this is consequently investigated in the next chapters, xv to xviii, of the First Book of the "Topica".

An ethical concept like "anger" must be deconstructed into affect and legitimate emotion, as Aristotle does in his "Nicomachean Ethics", and it must further be deconstructed into types of affects in relation to types of external causes and internal states. Similarly anger must be investigated in relation to social obligations, values, and emotional bonds. Aristotle's point of view is that there is a legitimate anger based on reason, and the result of careful deliberation, because its causes are the violation of the just. A canonical example would be the anger felt by an employee towards his immediate manager. This anger could be unjust or just viewed from without. The problem is that the protreptic guide should not deal with the moral and ethical problems of anger directly, and should not at all conceive of it as a projection, etc. The questions posed must be: "What is anger?" and the answers most likely to drive the conversation on would be ones like "I feel that there is a sense in anger!", or "I find anger irrational!" The point is that anger ought not to be grasped in the tempting mirror of functionality, instead its emotions and passions must be experienced in their depth under the perspective: "What does anger do to my life?", or "Am I my anger, or is it something alien which derives me of power?" This is the Greek legacy of conceiving the passions.

We must however not forget that the Greek "bible" the "Iliad" sets out with a eulogy of the anger of Achilles. This is the perspective of the warrior and broadly irrelevant to us today.

One way to start the process of investigation into the meaning of words, as suggested by Aristotle in chapter xv of the First Book of the "Topica", is to seek its contrary. If there are differences among the contraries the concept itself will be equivocal. The contrary of "confidence" is "suspiciousness", but also "mistrust", "indifference", "haughtiness", and "cynicism". Then confidence has different meanings. It can be the result of an open hearted attitude, it can be a strategy, and it can be obtained through a thorough knowledge of the other, or chosen in spite of such knowledge. Mistrust can be a trait of character, or a rational reaction in an event, and thus confidence can be based on both a positive, unconscious attitude towards others, and the result of a deliberate effort to develop a virtue. The same equivocation could be attributed to the capacity to recognize, to appreciate, to care, to love, to despise, and to hate ... and probably to every concept of inter-relational attitudes.

As Aristotle remarks, equivocation could be further differentiated when a distinction between the senses is reflectively absorbed in the use of a word. Relating to a tone the word "clear" has only a few contrary concepts, as "muffled", "with blurred intonation", or perhaps "feeble", but relating to color it has a lot: "dim", "vague", "indeterminable", "shimmering", etc.

I should remind you that propositions are *contradictories* when they must have opposite truth-values, that is, one must be true and the other false. For example, "The Eiffel Tower is high, the Eiffel Tower is not high".

Propositions are *contraries* when they cannot all be true. For example, "The Eiffel Tower was low" and "The Eiffel Tower was high" are contraries.

As regarding contraries they are also complicated in relation to ethical terms – contradictories are irrelevant here. The opposite of love might be hate, but if charity is meant by love, the opposite is indifference or selfishness, contempt or encroachment. If love between two persons is the meaning, less direct oppositions arise, like clinging to a person, making a person a habit, and being jealous, suspicious, and practicing the many types of intimate control. Further, the opposite of happiness might not be grief or sorrow; it might also be a depressing, tedious or cheerless state of mind, "nausea", "spleen", the catholic sin "acedia", and so on. The opposite of pleasure is generally seen as pain, but dispensing from the fact that pain might cause some sort of pleasure, pleasure itself is of so many kinds that its opposite might as well be "un-contemplative", or lacking desire, or initiative; and being without insight, wisdom of life, Modus Vivendi, proper culture (without it so many dimensions of life are lost), and not being loved by anybody, etc. So oppositions are replaced by contraries. Hence, it is a part of the protreptic method to search for contraries in order to discover the "economy of the pleasure of happiness" in an individual mind. This could also be done by exploring the sense of the opposite, i.e. of pain and sorrow, presupposed tacitly by the individual.

To be able to suggest the relevant contrary to a subject which has appropriated importance during the dialogue is of great importance to the protreptic guide. Let us say that the leading word was "trust", and that the other person at some time mentions self-confidence. It is now pertinent to get beyond the usual conceptual connotations of this word by suggesting an opposite of particular relevance to the other person (as sensed by the protreptic guide). This could for example be resentment. This is because this word is not normally seen as the contrary of self-confidence, but could be, considering that the sense of being unjustly treated is due to a lack of a certain dimension of self-confidence, namely self-respect. Here, one would often think that resentment is a product of self-respect, but it need not be. So this might be a clue to the feeling of self in the other person, and hence, to the values guiding this self-feeling.

It is of course of enormous importance to anybody, but especially to the leader, to know which kinds of confidence and recognition, happiness and pleasure, he actually expects and realizes, in order to know himself. This might also be the first step on the road to understanding why he actually feels confident, and to recognizing why he wants, or really wants, to feel this way.

Therapists would often guide this project by addressing the personal memory of experiences with these concepts, thus trying to establish a narrative genealogy of some kind. But protreptic only wants to follow the concept-analytical path, because narratives always create indirect approaches to values, often not just incorporating them, but blurring and distorting them by personal strategies of misconstruction. Exemplification is not always a short cut to the manifestation of sense and significance, be they ever so suggestive. One could state that narratives postpone the reflective labor on one's own values; however, it must be granted that in some cases they might be the only option to a break-through in dialogue (to use a martial metaphor).

It is important that the protreptic dialogue aims at discovering the reasons why a misconception of a concept, and hence, probably of the denoted value, exists (Rhe. II, xxiii, 24). Let us take "trustworthy". Any leader must be reliable, but cannot always be totally trustworthy. In everyday life trustworthiness depends on the capacity to be honest and to be sincere. However, trustworthiness manifests itself in a speech which appears frank, but which cannot reveal everything the leader knows in every situation. He might be obliged to hide something, for example due to loyalty to top management or to the board, or to protect groups or individuals. So reliability can neither be based on trustworthiness as total honesty, nor on sincerity. Knowledge has to be dosed, but the leader has a right to say that there is something which he cannot say. So it is wrong to demand that a leader should be completely trustworthy, even if he must be a reliable public servant; doctors and lawyers are subject to the same mental reservation.

However, this mental reservation does not count for the leader's relation to himself. One speaks about being honest to oneself, or sincere, but neither of being trustworthy, nor of being reliable to oneself. Thus it is presupposed that one does not want to hide something from oneself, and this is problematic, because we do that all the time at different levels of consciousness. So the protreptic investigator must search into this subject. Not by accusing the other person of lying to himself, but by suggesting the possibility of not being totally honest. Here the protreptic guide might use himself as an example.

It is important to find contradictions between that which the addressed says that he does, and that which he actually does (Rhe. II, 23). However, the dialogue must not be led in order to expose the other person. The point is to get an acceptance of the possibility, and to find a contradiction at the level of understanding concepts, not at the level of intentions. This conclusion must be drawn by the other person himself in relation to himself. If he says that he is good at giving recognition, it could be asked both what he understands by recognition, and how he manages to give it, but the starting point is the acceptance of the truth of this statement.

There are two dramatic grips in the protreptic dialogue. The first one is that the other person must not be able to foresee the course of the conversation. Surprise is a very important technique, for example when the subject is freedom. The protreptic guide could ask about the etymology of the word. Actually to be free means to be among kin, i.e. protected by a group. Interesting when everybody seems to think that one sense of freedom consist in breaking with your background. Such a break is normally impossible if anything other than establishing oneself in relation to a new group. The other dramatic grip is the musical course of the conversation, approaching a climax through the elaborations of value-themes, and either ending just after the climax, e.g. deliberately barring a proper finish, or letting the dialogue hover in paradox or dilemma. This is because the dialogue proves its worth by continuing its work inside the other person long after it has ended. At the best the dialogue must produce afterthought, deep reflections, and modes of discovering something about oneself, and even if there sometimes appear a break-through in the conversation, sudden insights, and incidents of alternative reflection, and even if emotional watersheds are reached, what really was obtained in the dialogue must be fulfilled by the other person himself. One can say that the protreptic guide borrows the receiver his voice, but that it is the task of the receiver to use it for his inner dialogue   I am often asked whether it is recommended to use metaphor or simile deliberately in the protreptic dialogue. The answer is that it is allowed when the conversation has become deadlocked. Aristotle calls the metaphor "a kind of enigma" (Rhe. III, ii, 12), and values can be described through metaphor, not only because the words which refer to them often have a metaphorical basis, but because a metaphor is able to open the meaning and the signification of a value. "Responsibility", for example, is documented 1836 in the modern sense, but was imported as a root into English as "response" around 1300 from Latin "responsum", "answer". But it is probably a word from the court, and hence, a way in which an accused defends himself, in such a manner that he is believed and spoken free. It also has the connotation of consciousness in the will and capacity to give answer by one voice of the "I", I-1, to a calling, summoning, or questioning, and accusation from another inner voice with a moral authority, I-2 (We are almost able to visualize I-1 and I-2 before the judge, the Third I). So consciousness, as Immanuel Kant showed in his *Anthropology*, is based on the metaphor of the court.

If responsibility is the subject of a protreptic dialogue, then the protreptic guide might ask the other person if his inner dialogue is about responsibility, and about how he experiences hes inner space or "room", and the forensic agents.

A common technique in therapy and coaching is to ask about a metaphor describing the situation of the other person. If the protreptic guide uses this trick, he must as quickly as possibly ask about the values connected to it, and not ask about the psychological qualities implied by it. If the respondent should say "I feel like a swallow", the guide could ask "does that mean lightness, detachment, or the ability to survey your own life?" If the answer is the last one, the guide could ask "What do you accomplish by that?" Whatever the answer is, it is likely that it will connect to the other person's relation to power, and hence, it will reveal something about his evaluation of the role of other people in his life.

The reflections on responsibility can often reveal, how the receiver relates to his own past, i.e. through his criteria and values. It would be a typical mode to proceed in protreptic, if the guide then asks "What is a person's past?" If the issue is responsibility, the answer shall reveal how he as a person manages the question of guilt, especially if he is able to take responsibility for that which happened, or conceives of himself as a victor or a victim. Guilt is not seen as a symptom or as a mental barrier in protreptic, but as a sign of maturity, unless it is very dominating or appears to be without proper reason.

It is extremely important that the protreptic guide is able to keep the dialogue at a high level of intensity. This is the goal of dialectic, and why he must be able to manage the trope. He must turn an answer around, or pose an unexpected question. Let us say that the subject is "personal development". If the other person claims that he does not experience any contradictions between his attempt to develop on his own terms and the value system or culture of the organization, a question could be. "Is it possible for you to understand your own terms?" or "Why do you evade the confrontation?" or "Do you have a corporate personality?"

If the other person claims that his job gives him the optimal opportunities to develop, the protreptic guide could ask: "What is an optimal opportunity?" The other person might then answer: "The basic challenges!", and then the protreptic guide could follow up by asking: "What is a basic challenge? Is it one which is sufficient? Is it something which you know you are able to do? Or is it something, which you do not know whether you are able to?" The other person might then answer: "Something of both!" Then the protreptic guide could go on: "What is it in you that develops? Is it your inner human being or your professional character? I myself have felt caught precisely in this dilemma." The other person might answer: "Both. They develop at the same time." Again the protreptic guide might ask: "How do you know that?" The other person might answer: "I have a gut feeling." Here the protreptic guide must persist and ask: "Then you seem to know who or what your inner human being is? But I must confess that I am a bit suspicious about my own gut feeling!" "What else do you have to navigate after?" the other person might say. "I believe more in reflection," the protreptic guide could answer. If then the other person replies that he does not think that reflection is more reliable than gut feeling, the dialogue has been very well led, and the protreptic guide can ask: "What do you find deceptive about reflection?" The other person might answer, "It is the sincerity of my inner voices." "But isn't there something inside you who listens to these voices in order to find some truth?" "Perhaps," the other might answer, "but this "listening something" might also deceive me!" We are now inside the scenario of Descartes. "After all," the protreptic guide could say, "you can look at your own actions. They will show you something about how you think and feel!" "Why," says the other person, "they might be strategic too!" "So our being is just an experiment which we perform with ourselves?" the protreptic guide might conclude. "No," says the other person, "existence is too precious for that." "This means that there is something which you cannot do or even must do?" asks the protreptic guide. "I think so." says the other person. "Could this limit or urge be called your values?" asks the protreptic guide. "Perhaps" says the other person. "Are you able to name just one of these values?" the protreptic guide asks. Normally the answer will be positive, for example "fairness".

From here the protreptic guide could easily go on and say "How do you know that". If the answer is "My gut feeling" then it would be too sophist-like to ask again "What is a gut feeling?" Instead the protreptic guide could say "Is there not a value more basic behind fairness?" The recipient says perhaps "What do you mean?" "Let us take the example that fairness is applied in a concrete situation in relation to a group of employees, then we must know what is the right thing to do" the protreptic guide says. "Is it fair to treat everybody alike, or is it allowed to treat differently the performance of one or two?" "It depends on what they have accomplished" I should think answers the recipient. "All right, but if we know that everybody tried seriously, but only one or two succeeded, should the whole group be emphasized instead of the few?" "The whole group" answers the recipient. "But is this just?" The protreptic guide asks. "Oh, I see" says the recipient, "you think of justice?" "Indeed", answers the protreptic guide, "so let us speak about justice. For example, is it possible to be fair without being just?" "Oh, do you mean if fairness could be strategic?" the recipient answers. "Something like that," says the protreptic guide, "do you think that justice is an intention or only visible in the accomplished act?" "Yes" answers the recipient, "I recognize the dilemma, because it has happened that I thought I acted justly, but afterwards realized that my action was wrong." "Give an example, please" says the protreptic guide. "Sometimes a leader must act by intuition, and it happens that it is wrong. I felt forced to do something in the organizational context, which I might not have done as a private person."

As can be seen, the protreptic guide must simply go on until the other person either states something about the values of the self, the development of which is the real subject, or concedes that he does not know, or that this inner human being comes into existence by the very process of professional development in opposition to genuine human pretensions. Then again, the dialogue could be driven on by the question: "What is professional development then?" "Proficiency, virtuosity, ... you name it!" answers the other person. "Do they suffice for personal development? Where are the other human beings in this connection? Where is generosity, or is it not one basis of fairness?" the protreptic guide could go on. "Managers cannot afford to be generous" the receiver answers. "So fairness could be rule-based in a managerial context?" asks the protreptic guide. "Do you mean that it has some definite codes of conduct?" the receiver asks. "No" says the protreptic guide, "but in a professional context it is often interpreted thus, although proper justice means to act according to the spirit of the law, not according to its letter." "I think you might be right" the receiver says. "Do you then think that proper justice could be taught?" the protreptic guide asks. "I actually do not know" the receiver answers.

That the dialogue might end in a cul-de-sac or even in paradox is exactly the point, and the moment has come when the conversation must be brought to an end. It is then up to the other person to give himself the answer afterwards.

Thus, the protreptic dialogue must deliver the intensity of questioning one's own life as a task of the other person. The aim is not to make him desperate, but to urge him to set himself free through self-knowledge. The goal is never frustration, but freedom. This could be effected as far as the problems rendered are universal and hence, non-personal or anonymous—they are the questions anyone could and ought to ask himself. In a world where organizations seem obliged to produce sense-making, the predicaments, unpredictability, and even absurdity of this task could be revealed.

The protreptic guide must have a very highly developed sense of the other person. He must be a virtuoso of empathy. How this is done must be the personal problem of the protreptic guide. There is no curriculum of empathy except experience and good will – courses in the reading of body language come close to the absurd.

The protreptic must care absolutely for the other person. Thus he must be sincerely kind, and his task is to assist the other, never to judge him. However, what happens in the protreptic dialogue could be almost catastrophic if the protreptic guide at any moment loses control of what is happening, or feels something that cannot be controlled approaching, and does not act in due time. He must be utterly on guard for the smallest reactions of the other person in order to change the course of dialogue.

The subject of the conversation is always the event of dialogue. The attentiveness towards the event as a mutual product of the interlocutors is of utter importance. The reflective processes produced must always be seen as situated in a socio-economic context, and values must be interpreted thus. The protreptic guide must be the facilitator of the recognition of the event as a process of liberation.

12.

Protreptic as the art of liberation as an event

Some reflections on the semantics of the event

As has been said already, the concept of the event originates in the Latin word "eventum", which is a translation from the Greek concept of "pragma", a word with quite a lot of important references indeed. Again, as already mentioned, "pragma" in the *Poetics* of Aristotle means "plot", but in the overall, classical Greek tradition it is the word for action, for doing, a related substantive being "praxis". However, in the epistemology of Aristotle it means "an object", and in the vocabulary of the Stoics, it means "the sense of that which happens".

The "pragma" circumscribes the three fold sense of the capacity to happen: The necessary, the contingent, and that of which we could claim or accept the responsibility. Let us have this philosophical relation in mind. The event, the "eventum", appears in the context of managerial thinking as that which could be managed, i.e., planned and controlled, either through model-theoretic prediction, through strategic instruments, or through a mixture of situated and generalised intuition. This effort of management is thus both applied at the cognitive level through this very anticipation and prediction, and at the practical level, through the ability to enforce their implementation. Also the event has become an important element of the experience economy (e.g., professional event planning). However these strategic uses only refer to a small aspect of the event, and as perspectives they are rather misleading, because so few events can really be controlled.

As an alternative to these concepts of the event we have first the occurrence, and second, the incident. I do not find that the concept of "situation" was ever an option here as a terminus technicus, because it presupposes the intellectual distance of the effort of reflection, and as such, it has been an important concept in the "decisionist" framework of Sartre's existentialism. An occurrence, however, seems to relate to minor aspects of a greater process of happening, or to something relatively unimportant. The incident, on the other hand, offers a more serious alternative. The mental aspect of the incident, "aliquid mihi incido in mentem", "something comes to my mind", and the physical process of prevention: "nisi si quid inciderit", "so that nothing shall happen" are both of great impact to our lives. In the terminology presented here the incident would differ from occurrence and accident in the fact that in the incident we are objects of the process of happening to the highest degree. We can both be responsible of accidents and occurrences at some level of consciousness, but hardly, I think, of incidents.

If we construct the diairetic structure of the event, it could look like this – here we must consider that the now is timelessness inside time, and that the moment is time outside time:

To happen

The moment: time outside time

The event

To take place

The now: The point inside time

Incident accident occurrence

dialogue

Things happen to my mind and to my body. Things happen. When they are said to "take place", they are already allocated.

The relation to the event is prediction, anticipation, preventing, furthering, and control, but also to give chance a chance. If philosophy shall insist on its own powers, it must not only be able to present us with a unique answer to the question "What happened?", thus coming dangerously close to the science of history, but it must above all be able to answer the question: "What does it mean to happen?"

The answer to both questions is "The fact of happening did happen".

If we accept this Zen-like answer, we also accept the unique position of philosophy. If we grant this to philosophy, we give it the right to be a privileged meta-language of the process of happening – I could be tempted to replace the concept of "taking-place" for "happens", because events so often are named after places, but I shall not deal with the issue of naming the event further here.

Firstly, a primary philosophy (a proto-philosophy) should be able to substantiate its own conceptual project. It would thus seem to be uninfluenced by its process of happening. As an act of contemplation, thinking is seen as a venture beyond any influence of the event in the Western philosophical history. Whatever happens, you would still be able to think the same. Thinking is sameness, happening is otherness. This would mean that philosophy could move in a direction opposite to time. In thinking the event, we create the un-eventual. Or, if we let go of the claims of a primary philosophy, it would mean quite the contrary, namely that thinking itself as a process is caught inside the "endechomenon", in that which could be otherwise – the early Christian philosopher, Boethius, who phrased the Latin word "contingere" for "chance", translated two concepts from Aristotle, the "endechomenon", "that which is possible without being necessary", and the "symbainein", "the throw", "the "facticity" of happening", into "contingency", so it means "the uncontrolled possibility which we make real by acting it out". Thinking then would be an incident parallel to the event which it tries to catch through words and phrases, ever doomed to try to catch the present up, but hurled behind its back into the past. This is what Merleau-Ponty meant by hyper-dialectic or hyper-reflection as mentioned earlier.

No doubt, taking the event seriously, we must admit that the event of thinking is an event, or at the most an event in an event, and hence, not an event which could be reflectively controlled, even if it could be more or less carefully prepared, and more or less goal-directed. In spite of strict logic, coherence, and axiomatic pretensions, thinking is not able to give the cause of, nor to be the reason for, thinking. There exists no place outside the event from where to give a priori definitions of eventing except the event itself, and this produces a circulus vitiosus. However, considering the event as the real subject of experiencing and thinking, we could speak about a positive self-reference given by the fact that thought happened. This destroys the common logic of philosophy, but opens a new field of insight into the connection between thinking and being.

So it seems that we can neither escape the fact of being "evented" in the very process of thinking, nor the fate of being let out of this event. We cannot escape this, but we can think the un-eventual in the possibility of thinking about the happening of that which happens.

The un-eventual is synonymous to the concept of the *moment.*

The moment is a peculiar mixture of the a priori and the a posteriori. We cannot define time by the hand of time. However, we seriously sense that time is more than the second, more than an empty passage from the future to the past, more than the physicists' mathematical point.

Since Plato's dialogue *Parmenides*, "to exaiphnes", the sudden, but also the process of happening as a space in time, or before, or beyond time, has been different from "ho nun", the point of the nano-second, the head of the needle, through which the future is transformed into the past, the "chainein", the chasm, of Chronos. It has been closer to the "kairos", "the right moment", celebrated in Greek rhetoric tradition as the "now" of happiness, the "fruit of the "kairé", and even closer to "the pleroma" of St. Paul, "the fulfilled time", "the union of the manifold in Christ", carried on through the non-Christian Plotius and the church-father Sc. Augustine, seeking the place where eternity and time intersects, where the mind of God and the mind of man could touch on the inner side of being. It got its final dichotomic articulation in the scholastic philosophers of the Middle Ages, who distinguished between "nunc permanens", and "nunc stans", between the moment of eternity filled with all time, and the moment of compressed, or condensed time, the "contractio" or "complicatio" (fold) of Nicolaus Cusanus. Later on the "nunc stans" of Meister Eckehart was developed into the moment of Pascal and of Kierkegaard, and in more modern

philosophy, in the quasi-profane dimension inspired by evolutionary theory and by depth psychology, and taken into possession by
Bergson, Husserl, Benjamin, Heidegger and Deleuze as "duration",
"duré" being not just the opposite of the flux of time but of linearity and simultaneity. Here we have the concept of the moment as
that which is lasting, as a flow, a streaming beyond time, or exactly
on the edge of time being neither depth nor surface. The "duatio"
in Latin; the "diastema" in the Greek comes close to this sense, or
the "periferontes" of Epicurus. The moment is the crack between
Being and The Being, the agent of the ontological difference, but
also the negation of this very difference, its breaking out of this
very confinement as that which denies the concept by hand of it.
The moment is the pure gesture in which the Being presents being
through a reciprocal absorption, the un-instantiated, the unique,
the proper "untimely".

It is not of small importance that the original sense of "be"
is to "become" in Proto Indo European, and the amalgamative
history of this verb is of great interest. The "Online Etymology
Dictionary", Douglas Harper, 2001 writes:

*"Be", from O.E. beon, beom, bion "be, exist, come to be, be-
come," from P.Gmc. *beo-, *beu-. Roger Lass ("Old English")
describes the verb as "a collection of semantically related paradigm fragments," while Weekley calls it "an accidental conglom-
eration from the different Old English dial[ect]s." It is the most
irregular verb in Mod.E. and the most common. Collective in
all Gmc. languages, it has eight different forms in Mod.E.: BE
(infinitive, subjunctive, imperative), AM (present 1st person
singular), ARE (present 2nd person singular and all plural),
IS (present 3rd person singular), WAS (past 1st and 3rd persons singular), WERE (past 2nd person singular, all plural;
subjunctive), BEING (progressive & present participle; ger-
und), BEEN (perfect participle). The modern verb represents
the merger of two once-distinct verbs, the "b-root" represented
by be and the am/was verb, which was itself a conglomerate. The
"b-root" is from PIE base *bheu-, *bhu- "grow, come into being,
become," and in addition to Eng. it yielded Ger. present first and
second person sing. (bin, bist, from O.H.G. bim "I am," bist*

"thou art"), L. perf. tenses of esse (fui "I was," etc.), O.C.S. byti "be," Gk. phu- "become," O.Ir. bi'u "I am," Lith. bu'ti "to be," Rus. byt' "to be," etc. It is also behind Skt. bhavah "becoming," bhavati "becomes, happens," bhumih "earth, world."

The word "being" as the expression of the "presentification" of the moment by a self-conscious existent person through a sense of duration gives the moment a peculiar position in relation to the event, because it is both its background, its possibility, and the force which destroys it – since being connotes becoming. If we conceive of the moment as the arena of the event, as its shadow, or as its screen, we position ourselves outside it, and this is of course an aporia. We are always inside a moment, but a moment which both is inside an event, and which has the event inside it.

If contemplation, "contemplatio" in Latin, "theoria" in Greek, should render a place outside the event, it should equal the uneventual, but of course thinking happens too, insofar as it is performance, and insofar as we are neither able, nor probably want to be able, to fully control it – since we cannot think the "noesis noeseoes" from Aristotles *Metaphysics,* the thought of thought.

Nevertheless, the non-eventual must exist, it must be more than a phantasm. This is the lesson from Plato, especially from the dialogue Parmenides, and from all "healthy" metaphysics: We cannot think the concepts of difference, Otherness, movement, manifold, without having a concept of the One and the Same. We must be able to think the event as having a dimension, a refuge, from where thinking could take off, even if it can never be the master of its own basis.

But how does it exist?

It would be a great fault to identify it with necessity. Necessity seen at a higher level is equal to chance. Chance is nothing but the inability to overlook the laws and causes of that which happens as cosmic or macro events themselves.

The un-eventual is not a quality at the material level, however theoretical profound the ascription is. The un-eventual can only be due to a capacity of holding an attitude. It must, then, be produced by our mind as an intentional object. The un-eventual then, is similar to the process of being able to be able. I shall call this a *proto-capacity.* The proto-capacity is the capacity to create the event of being-able-to. Nicolaus Cusanus named it "possest", to be able to be, or, I am that I can. The program of Merleau-Ponty sounds in this Latin neologism.

I am inclined to claim that the capacity of "being able to be able" is similar to a state of mind, and hence to an attitude. A state of mind has an intrinsic relation to the moment in two dimensions: It lasts in a way beyond chronological time. And it cannot be reduced in any way, i.e. it is immune to analytical reflectivity, or, it works through a positive self-reference.

Here the difference between accident or incident and event presents itself immediately: we can relate to an event as a function of the cooperation between the moment and our state of mind, hence we can receive the event with the very same gesture through which we create it; but we can neither deliberately create the accident nor be master of the incident, we can only suffer it. However, we can be prepared for both.

The event and the incident coincide in one important aspect: This proto-capacity opens the door to our being able to be able to let the incident be through its transformation into an event. This is being turned onto itself; the capacity to let the ability to be *be*. But to let the capacity of letting being be itself, *be*, is the same as a certain way of doing.

It seems that we can do philosophy. Doing philosophy is letting being be.

The basic attitude towards the event

Well, the leadership of the event is the proto-capacity to let being be as an event. This might sound like Heidegger, but the reference is Hellenistic philosophy – from which also Heidegger inherited the most important aspects of his way of thinking. However, it must definitely neither be understood as a tacit program of passivity, nor as the expression of superiority in relation to all other human beings, and in it we must not see the megalomania of the ultimate wise man – as Pascal did, when he criticized the Stoics lack of piety. To be able to receive the event does not mean to follow the man who seems strong enough to become the master of it, quite the opposite, it means both to suffer the slings and arrows of outrageous fortune or to take arms against a sea of troubles – to quote from "Hamlet". Epicurus says in his famous letter to Monoeceus, one of the most well-known protreptic texts from antiquity, as quoted by Diogenes Laertius, that the wise has the following relation to destiny:

> *"Destiny, which some introduce as sovereign over all things, he laughs to scorn, affirming rather that some things happen of necessity, others by chance, others through our own agency. For he sees that necessity destroys responsibility and that chance or fortune is inconstant; whereas our own actions are free, and it is to them that praise and blame naturally attach"*[22]

Now, the things which happen through our own agency are things which are inside the range of our own power. The Greek concept is "ta ef' hemin", "in nostra potestate" in Latin. Aristotle also refers to this important line of demarcation in the first book of his "Art of Rhetoric", when he develops the concept of the deliberative speech. He says:

> *"We must first ascertain about what kind of good or bad things the deliberative orator advises, since he cannot do so about everything, but only about things which may possibly happen or not (endechetai kai genésthai kai mé). Everything which of necessity either is or will be, or which cannot possibly be or come to pass, is outside the scope of deliberation. Indeed, even in the case of things that are possible, advice is not universally appropriate; for they include certain advantages, natural and accidental (fúsei enia kai apo túches), about which it is not worthwhile to offer advice. But it is clear that advice is limited to those subjects about which we take counsel; and such are those which can naturally be referred to ourselves and the first cause of whose origination is in our power (he arche tes genéseos ef' hemin estin); for our examination is limited to finding out whether such things are possible or impossible for us to perform (dunata e adúnata praxai)."*[23]

---

22 Diog.Laert. "Lifes of Eminent Philosophers", Loeb, Vol II, 133.
23 Op.cit. I, iv, 2-3.

The ability to let being be deals with the capacity to distinguish between that which is in our power, that which we can produce, prevent, or change, and that which is not. Necessity and chance are realms outside our power. However, this must not be misunderstood in such a way that we cannot act within the realm of the necessary, the realms of laws, the "tynchanon", but only that there are effects of these laws which we cannot influence, even if we try. It must be obvious that this line is fluid.

To let the event be by co-creating it, means to be able to base our practice on this distinction. Incidents, hence, are, like accidents, intensities in the flow of happening, which are not inside our own power, but as a species of what is happening they might be mastered in due time. The event is that which we are able to influence. Here we can sense an ethos of the event, because we can transform an incident into an event by letting being be. If we anticipate – the "parascheué", the "anticipatio" of Epictetus – of the incident, and confront that which occurs, as if it were exactly what we had wished for, we are able to transform the incident into an event.

Let us take an example of a trivial incidence: You lose your car keys. This could not properly be called an accident, since it would only be so, or a part of one, if the use of the car keys were urgent because of an ill family member, etc. Instead of being irritated, resenting, just make the best plan to find them, or to get some new ones. Then learn from it by imaging a life without a car, and be happy or unhappy about having one, and reflect why it is so.

Letting the event be is, however, not a mental attitude which must produce defeatism. Because it demands an effort of the intellect to be able to draw the demarcation line between that which is in our power, and that which is not. This means that we must learn to play a greater part. The more we know about the laws of action, about the economic and social structures, and about history, the more we are able to push this demarcation line in our favour. Even if our methods of describing necessity in the domains of science, and pseudo-science (macro economics), and our practices of planning and prediction, might produce new frontiers of powerlessness, we cannot renounce knowledge. Even if our attempts to cope with chaos might seem disastrous sometimes, we could at least learn from them. "This is the place from which we start: Men shall know commonwealth again from bitter searching of the heart" – to quote Frank Scott and Leonard Cohen, we must "rise to play a greater part" in order to make the world ready for the event.

If the leadership of the event means to let being be, it also demands that we confront the way in which being manifests itself in the regional ontologies, which Husserl spoke about. Or to put it otherwise, in order to let being be, we have to develop the "krinein", the critical attitude in relation to the being of being. But "krinein", the "kritiké" of the intellect, in its special mixture between socially and historically mediated capacity and universal force, cannot do without some non-subjective cornerstones of orientation. We have to navigate in relation to norms about the Good, the Just, the True, the Beautiful, and Freedom.

The alternative would have the consequence that this capacity to let being be would develop into a cult of authenticity. The cult of authenticity represses the fact that being is mediated through language and that language always belongs to others. Language is the effect of a never ending combat between objects and bodies, and the relations among them, of minds on the one side, and situated – or shall we say "evented" – consciousness on the other.

A pure, reflective attitude towards the things which happen focused on developing oneself into an individual in total command of its own affections would produce a sort of ethical or even of metaphysical narcissism, the Stoic ideal of the "katorthoma", the ultimate wise man which Pascal scorned for its lack of realism, and of humility, in his "Pensées". Put another way, the leadership of the event can never be based on the transcendental or self-sufficient ego. We must realise that the being of being is produced by Otherness. This means that the being of being is always alienated. But alienation could, however, be a positive concept. In love it certainly is, since the capacity to make the other's mind transparent would destroy love's labour and the chances taken, and hence the passion aroused by the unpredictability and mystery of the other.

The event could be seen as the arena of a productive alienation. Productive alienation means that we can only speak about that which is in *our* power. It is a question of the character of the *We* and, hence, of the *Us*. I have already given positive alienation a concept, I called it *the principle of translocutionarity*.

To transform the incident into an event, and, hence, to develop the platform of the leadership of the event, is to be able to let being be as the being of the Other. I have named this attitude *heteroenticity* in opposition to authenticity. It means to relate to oneself through the Other, "heteros", in the Greek, and through Otherness (See the chapter on symmetry).

So, the leadership of the event must mean the ability to create a balance between my own intentionality and the foreign intentionality of both the other persons and of the event itself. I am addressed, summoned, called for, and I am obliged to answer. Real leadership of the event is about being able to receive, which is the concealed content of the word "capacity";"capacitas" in Latin is a translation of the Greek term "dechomein", "to take", but also "to receive", "to recognise", "to accept a gift, "to welcome" and "to host". "Dechomein" is also translated into the Latin concepts of "recipio" and "suscipio", and what are "receptiveness" and "susceptibility" but "letting being be"? This attitude contains a dialectic of taking and giving, a dialectic which forms the core of heteroenticity. To speak and to listen, to listen and to speak, the chiastic bond of another presence, a presence always alienated, but anyhow always pure; a presence on behalf of otherness.

The concept of the protreptic dialogue presupposes a theory of the event. The dialogue is a species of the event as genus, just as the event is a species of the genus combining the duration in time and the tension between the limitation of place (topos) and the infiniteness of space or "space-ness" (chora), a genus which could be named happening or "taking-place".

The concept of event can then be seen as both a genus and as a species (we have already showed that). As a species it could be an instance of more concepts, as mentioned above: aspects of time like the moment, duration, or the opposite (the now without extension in time), or movement, becoming, or history, but most likely of "taking-place". As a genus it would refer to the species accident, incident, occurrence, case, happening, or to the result of deliberate or planned action versus the opposite. Sub-species would be disaster, catastrophe, gathering, meeting, venue, lecture, party, coitus, combat, and hazard ..., the list is very long.

But seen from a certain angle the event is a unique being, a thing without a more definite species and a genus; Aristotle uses the word "species" in this connection, since he thinks that all that exists must have a genus: "when we cannot find any higher term apart from the individual" ("kath' hekaston")", Posterior Analytics, I, v, 5. Anything which has a name belongs virtually to a species, but might not do it concretely. This means that its type cannot be decided precisely. When two people meet apparently unexpectedly, and they happen to fall in love, is this meeting a casual accident or something due to some aspect of deliberate action? It is perhaps named "our first meeting", but this does not identify it properly as a species, insofar as this is due to the fact that it is totally dependent on the individual actually or potentially (by being told, and in the future) experiencing it. This means that while its species cannot be decided unambiguously, its genus can, insofar as it is an event. Anyhow we could also conceive of a meeting as a sub-species of the species "event", and hence refer to both duration and becoming as the genus. So either the concrete event is indefinite as an event – one does not know what took place, only that something happened – or has an identity as a species, but its sense is preliminary, since what it is, will not appear until later (the meeting produced an unsuccessful marriage, and hence what seemed to be a stroke of good luck was a hidden disaster). Hence, the event is a species which could refer to becoming as its genus in such a way that naming subsumed under a species must be hypothetical.

Let us further investigate the etymology of the concepts of happening:

Etymologically the concept of "event" can be traced back to 1573, from M.Fr. event, from L. eventus "occurrence, issue," from evenire "to come out, happen, result," from ex- "out" + venire "to come". Eventually "ultimately" first recorded c.1680; eventuality is 1828, originally "the power of observing in phrenology." Eventful is from 1600. Event horizon in astrophysics is from 1969.[24]

The species of event, "accident" can be traced back to 1374, meaning "an occurrence, incident, event," from O.Fr. accident, from L. accidentum (nom. accidens, gen. accidentis), prp. of accidere "happen, fall out," from ad- "to" + cadere "fall". Meaning

---

24 Online Etymology Dictionary, November 2001, Douglas Harper.

grew from "something that happens, an event," to "something that happens by chance," then "mishap."

The species of event, "incident", can be traced back to 1412, meaning "something which occurs casually in connection with something else," from L. incidentem (nom. incidens), prp. of incidere "happen, befall," from in- "on" + -cidere, comb. form of "cadere" "to fall". The sense of "an occurrence viewed as a separate circumstance" is from 1462. Meaning "event that might trigger a crisis or political unrest" first attested 1913. Incidental "casual, occasional" first recorded in Milton (1644). Conversational use of incidentally for "by the way" is first attested in 1925.

The species "occur" can be traced back to 1527, meaning "meet, meet in argument," from M.Fr. occurrer, from L. occurrere "run to meet, run against, befall, present itself," from "ob" "against, toward" + currere "to run". Sense development is from "meet" to "present itself" to "appear" to "happen" ("present itself in the course of events"). Meaning "to come into one's mind" is from 1626.

The species "happen" can be traced back to c.1300, "happenen" "to come to pass, occur," originally "occur by hap"; replaced O.E. gelimpan, gesceon, and M.E. befall. First record of "happenstance" is 1897, formed from happening + circumstance. Happening in the sense of "spontaneous event or display" is from 1959.

The species "case" can be traced back to 1225, meaning "state of affairs," from O.Fr. cas "an event," from L. casus "a chance," lit. "a falling," from cas-, pp. stem of cadere "to fall," from PIE base *kad- "to fall" (cf. Skt. sad- "to fall down," Armenian "chacnum" "to fall, become low," perhaps also M.Ir. "casar" "hail, lightning"). The notion being "that which falls" as "that which happens." Widespread extended senses in law, medicine, grammar, etc. In case "in the event" is recorded from c.1340

To take one sub-species, "hazard", it goes back to 1167, from O.Fr. "hazard", "hazard" "game of chance played with dice," possibly from Sp. azar "an unfortunate card or throw at dice," which is said to be from Arabic "az-zahr" (for al-zahr) "the die." But this is doubtful because of the absence of "zahr" in classical Arabic dictionaries. Klein suggests Arabic "yasara" "he played at dice;" Arabic -s- regularly becomes Sp. -z-. The -d was added in Fr. in confusion with the native suffix -ard. Sense of "chance of loss or harm, risk," first recorded 1548; the verb sense of "put something at stake in a game of chance" is from 1530. Hazardous in the sense of "perilous" is from 1618.

We can follow some essential distinctions here in the species: Between necessity and chance, between standing alone and being accompanied by something else or put explicitly into a context, between presenting itself and being hidden, and between spontaneous and deliberate. The distinctions between being the result of, and involving, one or more actors, are not contained in the words, neither are the distinctions between past and future, nor between levels of duration. This might appear strange since they are more than properties (in Aristotle a property is named an "idion" when it is "something which does not show the essence of a thing but belongs to it alone and is predicated convertibly of it." I, v, 15) in Aristotle's sense from the "Topica", because they belong to events only, and perhaps even belonging to their definition. The simple explanation, however, is that they all are species of the event which in principle can befall anyone and they are all time-modi of presence as becoming. Hence, they infold present, future and past as indistinguishably "Oneness" which *happens us*: comprehension, fear, regret, satisfaction hope and the wake dizzy "lethe" of desire, "haplósis-henósis", virtual simplification, the greatest gift of the event.[25]

The ontological levels of the event

In order to examine the event, we are forced to begin with an ontological distinction between three levels of what it could mean that something "happens" or "takes place".

1. The non-aliud

There is an ontological and epistemological practice of immense importance to our lives which is the capacity to say: "*This* has

---

25 In New-Platonist thinking the "haplósis" means a process of self-development in which the mind is made simple, and so simple that it is able to partake in the "henósis", the elevation and absorption in God as outlined in the philosophy of Plotinus. The Latin version is "simplification" which means "made singular" and hence, "conceivable", "clear", "manageable". The "docta ignorantia" of Nicolaus Cusanus sounds through these concepts, of course. What I want to express is that the event as the moment makes a "profane" being one with being possible, an authenticity granted us from time and thus, contra-intuitively, from becoming. It is always already happening just by lived or by "being lived", unnoticed.

happened!" However, neither this wording, nor the conceptualisation of the event, nor the reflective understanding of the event in which *eventing* itself is articulated, can be the proper "this". The "cascades of actualisations" of which Deleuze speaks in "What is Philosophy" (p.128), might simply bounce off the event, be untimely, or – since we, so at least it seems at this point in history, are denied the predicates "false" and "true" – without sufficient power to grasp the process-character of taking place. The manifold aspects of the process which, by occurring, are immediately present, embodying the eventing force, might neither "fit" the wording of the event which anticipates only a few aspects of the process of eventing, nor can they be properly received by the attempt of a reflective conceptualization of the eventing of eventing. This is the fatal incompatibility, the delicate crack, between effectuating and being received, between that which happens, and its articulation in the games of truth. This crack is the fissure between *"the sense of the event"* and *"the event of sense"*.

If this crack is taken as a proto-ontological "phenomenon", it goes beyond the so called "ontological difference", because it defies the predicate of "Being". The core of "the Being" (*"ousia"*, *"essence"*), can never be "Being" (*"einai"*, *"esse"*) itself, insofar as this core is the event. This is exactly what makes the famous distinction by Heidegger – which he perhaps borrowed from Middle Age philosopher Bonaventura – directly misleading.

Even the bold expression of the event as something between the subjective and the objective, between a pure mental sphere and a pure material sphere, and which was captured already by the Stoic tradition in the concept of "lekton", the zone of inter-relational sense, cannot do justice to the fundamental ontological level of the event.

In order to understand this fact, I have used the beautiful phrase by Nicolaus Cusanus from his little "trialogue", "De li non aliud": "Non aliud non aliud est quam non-aliud": "The not other is nothing other than the Not-Other." (I prefer this translation).

The event as a genuine phenomenon, as "the taking place", can in relation to time and place be conceived as *non-aliud*, as that which is beyond Sameness, and hence, beyond both the concept of identity, and beyond its negation. *Non-aliud* is a term in language which defies any representational structure. It signifies that it can neither be defined by affirmation nor by negation. It is tempting to hypothesise that *non-aliud,* then, is mere duration without space, making the expression "taking-place" irrelevant, but *non-aliud* is beyond both time and space, it is mere happening without these forms of perception.

Hence, the *non-aliud* could be a way to grasp the concept of an *absolute immanence,* a mode of existence, which implies no distinction between "outside" and "inside", between thinking and the thought, and between subject and object in a process of time. The genuine event is a shape, which absorbs the knowing into the known. From its absolute immanence follows the definition "that it has everything outside itself, except the knowledge of having everything outside itself", but even this radical definition is too much bound to the connotation of an experiencing subject to express the "being" of *non-aliud* – which we actually could not name, nor speak about. The event is totally dependent and totally autonomous, at the same time. It excludes a subject of knowledge, and hence the possibility of an epistemology, and hence, an ontology.

The *"eventum tantum",* a concept used both by Heidegger and Deleuze, means "the great event" or "so much of the event". *Non-aliud* is the closest possible analogy, at an ontological and epistemological level, of the event, and of our relation to it as genuine happening. This concept transcends both ontology and epistemology, it forms a performative contradiction. And this is, or "must be", what Deleuze thinks about, when he writes:

> *"The event is not what occurs (an accident), it is rather inside what occurs, the purely expressed. It signals and awaits us." (The Logic of sense", P.149)*

and that

> *"Each component of the event is articulated or effectuated in an instant, and the event in the time that passes between these instants; but nothing happens within the virtuality that has only meanwhiles as components and an event as composite becoming. Nothing happens there, but everything becomes, so that the event has the privilege of beginning again when time is past." (What is ph. p. 156)*

Compare Alfred North Whitehead, from whom Deleuze got the inspiration and concepts for much of his philosophy, in his criticism of Locke in the book "Process and Reality":

> *"If he had grasped the notion that the actual entity "perishes" in the passage of time, so that no actual entity changes, he would have arrived at the point of view of the philosophy of organism (W's philosophy. OFK)."*[26]

And

> *"An event is a nexus of actual occasions inter-related in some determinate fashion in some extensive quantum ... The most general sense of the meaning of change is "the differences between actual occasions in an event"*[27]

The *eventum tantum* is the prototype of the event, the event that, in the most radical sense of the words, *"Never was"*, the event, which *"was Never"*.

"Never" originates in O.E. "næfre", compound of ne "not, no" (from PIE base *ne- "no, not;" see "un-" + æfre "ever.) Early used as an emphatic form of not (as still in "never mind"); "nevermore" is first attested c.1205; nevertheless is from c.1300. Old English, unlike its modern descendant, had the useful custom of attaching "ne" to words to create their negatives, as in "nabban" for "na habban" "not to have." It. "giammai", Fr. "jamais", Sp. "jamas" are from L. "iam" "already" + magis "more;" thus lit. "at any time, ever," originally with a negative, but this has been so thoroughly absorbed in sense as to be formally omitted. In Danish however, it origins in common Nordic "ne aldri gi", in which "ne" is the negation, "aldri" origins in "aldr", "age", and "gi" means "at all", thus the word means "no age at all". This is rich insofar as it both refers back and forward in time, and hence, beyond time.

It is actually rather consequential to think of the event as *"Never"*, because the event cannot be defined as a *diastema,* as "an in-between-in-time and space" – as Deleuze seems inclined to – as a *duration,* without being thought of as "The moment"

---

26 *Process and Reality.* Corrected edt. New York: the Free Press. 1985, p. 147.
27 (p. 80)

beyond time; or better, as the moment *in* time, which creates the experience of time.[28] The alternative is Heidegger's *"ek-stasis"*, where the moment, the duration, is either thought of as a passage between the past and the present, or as a sort of privileged point of reflection on the very flux of time in which it is absorbed. Both versions would amount to betrayals of the event, because the event is nothing but a mere duration beyond time. The event is totally empty, nothing happens at the core of the event, because it is beyond the time-structures presupposed by language. So, an image of the non-aliud inside time would be the nunc stans of Scholastic mysticism, the condensed, infolded infiniteness or eternity in one moment of experience – translated into "das Nun" by Meister Eckehart.

Only through creating a level of ontological and epistemological approach to the *eventum tantum* which presses at the limit of thought, is it possible to escape the two classical traps of thinking about the event, the trap of naturalism (historically shaped), and the trap of negotiation/consensus/sense-creation, into which Alain Badiou seems to fall in his book "Being and the Event".[29]

However, in spite of this criticism Alain Badiou takes a step to understand the event in this first book of his on the event, "Being and Event", when he says: That what counts is not just "how does one think non-being?" but also "how does one name non-being?" The proper name is neither the transcendent God nor some aspect of genuine presence, but the "un-presentation and the un-being of the one". Thus it cannot be interpreted in a Kantian way as a guaranty of the validity of sense impressions – which Badiou after all by following Deleuze must try to establish too.

However Badiou does not go far enough, because the event

---

28 Whitehead gives in "Process and realty" another definition of duration: "A complete region, satisfying the principle of "concrescent unison" will be called a "duration". A duration is a cross-section of the universe; it is the immediate present condition of the world in some epoch, … the immediate present of each actual occasion lies in duration" p. 125. And the use of duration of Bergson which is perhaps closer to mine: "This is to replace ourselves in pure duration, of which the flow is continuous, and in which we pass insensibly from one state to another: a continuity which is really lived, but artificially decomposed for the greater convenience of customary knowledge." *Matter and Memory*, p. 243.
29 Badiou A. (2006): *Being and Event*. New York: Continuum.

must be conceptually framed at several epistemological levels beyond the determination of its trans-ontological status, it must be seen as an active area of non-sense working in the midst of our experience; as "an empty place", as Roland Barthes once framed it in his magnificent book on Japanese culture.[30]

Following Badiou the event has no objective existence; but since it exhibits a distinctively reflexive structure, it only occurs through what Badiou calls an 'interpretative intervention' (p. 181). The event is called into existence through the subject who recognizes it, or who nominates it *as* an event, and keeps faithful to it. However, from this perspective only the acceptance of a material causal level could guarantee that the transformation of individual interpretations into narratives of a wider sense, like the one of the French Revolution, would be more than the results of negotiations of nothing, i.e. of a phantasm of consensus.

The alternative is that the event indeed becomes a "phantasma" ("simulacra" in Latin) per se. So, in some sense it must be meaningful to state that the event does not exist. But this demands another level of ontology than the first one presented here which was *level-1, the eventum tantum as non-aliud.*

2. The alma-event

However, even the most radical philosophical approach has to have more capacities than just a negating aspect; it must have an affirmative dimension – which the concept of *non-aliud* does indeed have in spite of the context of the theologia negativa – that is also able to relate more directly to concrete phenomenological experience. Furthermore, we have to develop a concept that can serve as an antidote of sense to the general tendency to transform the event into a substantive often named after the place in which it happened and which projects the event into the past. We need another level, and this is, in my opinion, the level on which Deleuze operates. We need to be able to speak of the event as sense beyond sense, as an active, creative centre in the middle of our lives which we carry with us, and to which we are only able to relate to by "guarding its secret". Thus the event could be thought of as an empty place, a

---

30 Barthes R. (2006): *Empire of Signs.* Hill and Wang.

creative middle, "to méson", the golden centre of the globe in the philosophy of Parmenides, a phenomenon which can neither be described sufficiently as a material being through causal relations, nor spun as an intentional phantasm into the net of history.

At that level, there is a constant, hardly bearable tension in the middle of our lives, between the sense of the event – hard to bear because it is forced on us, either by other people or, alas, by our own experience, and by our memories – and the event of sense.

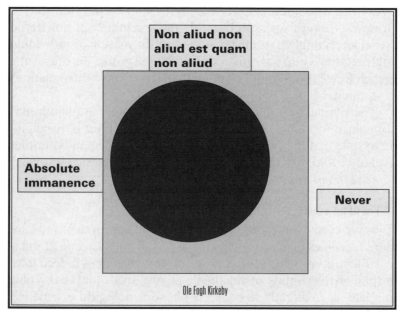

Fig. 5. Non-aliud[31]

Since the event of sense always must be allocated to "yet another event" as an experience, there must be an event of an immanently transcendent character, which is active in our life, but epistemologically inapproachable. It expresses a "positive self-reference", it is not an "never-ending regression", it is beyond time, or better, a

---

31 The following figures are paintings by the Russian Kasimir Malevich, the founder of suprematism from around 1915.

timeless time inside time, and hence, not even the possible subject of a "transcendental" reduction in the Kantian sense; but nevertheless it is certainly "there" in some sense, not just as the quasi-object of a constructional effort. The eventum tantum at this level, *level-2,* I name the *alma-event.*

The alma-event is the "non-place", the ouk-topos", of the event of sense. It is not a "noumenon", not "ein Ding an sich", because it is exactly not the silent and invisible guarantee of the possibility of the sense of the event. Rather, it is an "active nothing", an echo of an endless *Never* breaking into our lives. It is a thought without an object – as Hegel spoke about in "The Encyclopedia". Hence, it can only be thought *chiastically* (I shall evade the concept "dialectical") in relation to the sense of the event, as its permanent negation, as its core and its background, at the very same time, as its imago in the realm of "non-sense" – as Deleuze phrased it in "Logique de sens"

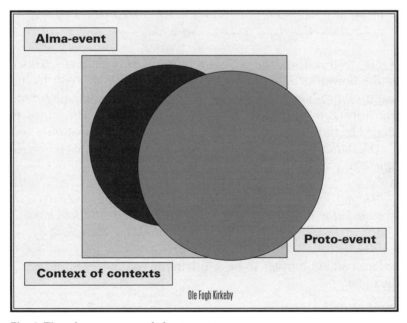

Fig. 6. The alma-event and the proto-event

111

3. The proto-event

The sense of the event, the most concrete level, would be called *"the proto-event"*. It lives a life between the ascribed sense of processes, and the total reification as occurring in the capacity of a thing: "The Davos-meeting", "a happy end", etc. The gliding on the surface of tension between the proto-event and the alma-event is expressed by Deleuze as the shift from substantive to verb, and in the verb itself, from the indicative to the infinitive. To Deleuze, the alma-event is already anticipated – *"parascheué"* in the Stoic terminology of Epictetus – by the very transformation in phrasing from "he dies" to "to die". That is why Deleuze is able to anticipate the alma-event by saying these already famous words:

> *"Every event is like death, double and impersonal in its double. It is the abyss of the present, the time without present with which I have no relation, towards which I am unable to project myself. For in it I do not die. I forfeit the power of dying. In this abyss they ("on") die – they never cease to die, and they never succeed in dying" (Log.o.Se. p.152)*

Hence, to transform the proto-event, the slowly sinking sparkles of the fireworks of sense, to the level of the alma-event, to the realm of productive non-sense, is the task of philosophy. This transformation includes "an ethos of the event". This ethos is shaped by the Stoic concepts of "parascheué", "anticipation", and *("synkatathasis")*, the ability to assent to everything that happens. Epictetus phrased it with genial simplicity:

> *"Do not seek to have everything that happens happen as you wish, but wish for everything to happen as it actually does happen, and your life will be serene." (Encheiridion, Paragraph 8).*

Deleuze allows himself to be a little more sophisticated in saying the same:

> *"There is a dignity of the event that has always been inseparable from philosophy as amor fati: being equal to the event, or becoming the offspring of one's own events – "my wound existed before me, I was born to embody it" (Log.o.Se. P. 159)*

THE WORDED EVENT IS STIGMATISED BY THE STORY, AND HENCE, THE CAUSALITY AND COHERENCY, IT IS INSCRIBED INTO

Ole Fogh Kirkeby

Fig. 7. The sense of the event

As already mentioned such a fidelity to and corporate intimacy with the event are not enough to create an ethos of the event.

To summarise: There are three levels on which to approach the event.

Level-1: The eventum tantum as non-aliud is beyond the capacities of ontology and epistemology, we can only hint at it by analogy – being aware, of course, of the performative self-contradiction in the very use of language, since the use of analogy presupposes both ontological and epistemological axioms.

Level-2 contains the tension between the sense of the event, the proto-event, and the event of sense, the alma-event. Since the alma-event is the core of every event, it is also the quasi-ontological *"topos"* as a "particularization" of the *"chora"*, of the possible worlds given by time and space. Perhaps this is what Deleuze meant by the "virtual" (a concept also inherited from Whitehead), where the other two concepts in this triad "the actual" and "the potential", on the other hand, belong to the realm of the proto-event.

113

Level-3 is the everyday level of the event, where incidents and occurrences are identified through a vocabulary ready at hand, and reified. It is here that the answer is given to the question: "What happened?", or "What actually happened?"No doubt, taking the event seriously, we must admit that the event of thinking is an event, or at the most an event in an event, and hence, not an event which could be reflectively controlled, even if it could be more or less carefully prepared, and more or less goal-directed. In spite of strict logic, coherence, and axiomatic pretensions, thinking is not able to give the cause of, nor to be the reason for, thinking. There exists no place outside the event from where to give a priori definitions of eventing exept the event itself, and this produces a circulus vitiosus. However, considering the event as the real subject of experiencing and thinking, we could speak about a positive self-reference given by the fact that thought happened. This destroys the common logic of philosophy, but opens a new field of insight into the connection between thinking and being. So it seems that we can neither escape the fact of being "evented" in the very process of thinking, nor the fate of being let out of this event. We cannot escape this, but we can think the un-eventual in the possibility of thinking about the happening of that which happens.

The un-eventual is synonymous with the concept of the *moment.*

The moment is a peculiar mixture of the a priori and the a posteriori. We cannot define time by the hand of time. However, we seriously sense that time is more than the second, more than an empty passage from the future to the past, more than the physicists' mathematical point.

Let us repeat the passage from page 94 about the phenomenon of duration:

Since Plato's dialogue *Parmenides*, "to exaiphnes", the sudden, but also the process of happening as a space in time, or before, or beyond time, has been different from "ho nun", the point of the nano-second, the head of the needle, through which the future is transformed into the past, the "chainein", the chasm, of Chronos. It has been closer to the "kairos", "the right moment", celebrated in Greek rhetoric tradition as the "now" of happiness, the "fruit of the "kairé", and even closer to "the pleroma" of St. Paul, "the fulfilled time", "the union of the manifold in Christ", carried on through the non-Christian Plotinus and the church-father Sc. Augustine, seeking the place where eternity and time intersects, where the mind of God and the mind of man could touch on the inner side of being. It got its final dichotomic articulation in the scholastic philosophers of the Middle Ages, who distinguished between "nunc permanens", and "nunc stans", between the moment of eternity filled with all time, and the moment of compressed, or condensed time, the "contractio" or "complicatio" (fold) of Nicolaus Cusanus. Later on the "nunc stans" of Eckhart was developed into the moment of Pascal and of Kierkegaard, and in more modern philosophy, in the quasi-profane dimension inspired by evolutionary theory and by depth psychology, and taken into possession by Bergson, Husserl, Benjamin, Heidegger and Deleuze as "duration", "duré" being not just the opposite of the flux of time but of linearity and simultaneity. Here we have the concept of the moment as that which is lasting, as a flow, a streaming beyond time, or exactly on the edge of time being neither depth nor surface. The "duratio" in Latin; the "diastema" in the Greek comes close to this sense, or the "periferontes" of Epicurus. The moment is the crack between Being and The Being, the agent of the ontological difference, but also the negation of this very difference, its breaking out of this very confinement as that which denies the concept by hand of it. If one for the sake of thought-experiment accepts that any abstraction must be able to be transformed through positive self-reference into a mental image – and hence subjected to time and space and the labour of the senses – we here have two constellations: one in which Being is seen either as the "nunc permanens" or as the "nunc stans", as unfolded or infolded/compressed time. This, however, does not do justice to the character of the "alma-event" as a concept without an image. The Being, on the other hand, is just a concept covering the wide range of representation from common sense to science. If the moment as duration shall neither be seen through the metaphor of the container nor through the one of the "flowing manifold", it has to conjure up a transgression of conceptual thinking. This is what is meant by calling it a "crack between Being and the Being", because it is the very constitution of the possibility of the distinction.

The moment is the pure gesture in which the Being presents

being through a reciprocal absorption, the un-instantiated, the unique, the proper "untimely".

Henri Bergson has made an original contribution in "Memory and Matter" to understanding the moment. He conceives of it as a duration different from the physical now-point. A duration that contains, as the experience of my present, the past as sensation and the future as movement, and the centre of which is sensori-motor, it is our body. So Bergson claims that the moment unites being and becoming. One consequence of his claim of the connection between movement and the future is that we are "before ourselves", which is corroborated by Benjamin Libet's famous research, and recently by Jeffrey Gray.[32]

As I see it, Bergson's claim that "... my present consists in the consciousness that I have of my body" is both right and wrong. It is right because we have a feeling of our body *in* the moment, or better, that our body *is* the presence of my present, but at the same "time" we are outside, or perhaps even "inside" time. Time does not stop during duration, it ceases to exist. There is neither consciousness of past nor future in the genuine moment. What *is* "during" duration is the event, and even if this has an internal flow, there is no externality, but an absorption by which we are physically suspended and so is our body. But logically, there must be a constant in all these flows and this is the moment itself, not the event. When the event is experienced as a substance, as a stasis with structure, as a "tode ti", this is due to the fact that the moment does not move. We become, but the moment is immoveable. It is the subject of being, we are not.

---

32 Op. cit. p. 176-180.Quote from p. 177. Gray and Libet claims that we become aware of willing an action only after the unconscious part of the brain causes it. Libet (1986) demonstrated that subjects show a readiness-potential for a 'willed' behavior before they report becoming aware of willing that behavior. From this he created the hypothesis that the unconscious part of the brain causes behavior independently of our conscious sensation of willing. To gauge the relation between unconscious potential of readiness and subjective feelings of volition and action, Libet required an objective method of marking the subject's conscious experience of the will to perform an action in time, and afterward comparing this information with data recording the brain's electrical activity during the same interval. See: Libet, B. (1985): "Unconscious cerebral initiative and the role of conscious will in voluntary action". *Behavioral and Brain Sciences*, 8: 529-566. And Gray, J. (2004): *Consciousness: Creeping up on the Hard Problem*. Oxford: Oxford University Press.

13.

The pentagon of the event

Now, the proto-event can be analytically systemised through the "elements" or the "zones of practice, experience, and knowledge" which constitute it, and are constituted by it. The guiding phenomenon and concept making this possible must be *the body*.

Thus, we can construct *the pentagon of the event:*

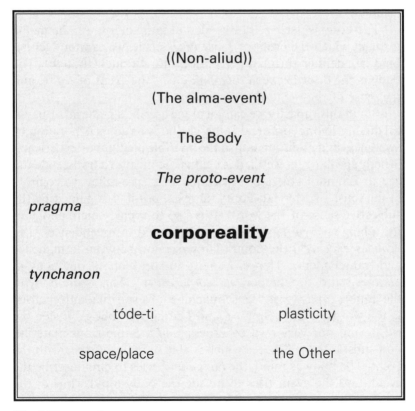

Fig. 4. The event

117

It is definitive that we are in the event only as bodies, whether through immediate experience, through memory, or through thinking. The body entrusts us to the event in the capacities of passionate things, things embodying a thinking desire and a desiring thought – as Aristotle put it in the *De anima*. We might of course "take part" in an event like a boxing match through TV, and this partaking is not physical in the genuine sense of the word, but it is bodily since it is conveyed through the senses. The concept of the audience complicates the relation between body and event, as in theatre and film, but epistemologically it can be coped with, as we are also able to relate conceptually to the fact of the purely imagined event. This is because these kinds of experiences are themselves events of perceiving events at a special or temporal distance.

The body is itself a transcendental immanence. As the media through which the event of sense takes place, we cannot "get behind it", neither through perception, nor through thought. The body is the door between the *alma-event*, the event of sense, and the sense of the event, the *proto-event*.

But in this capacity we cannot alone ascribe a material or physical quality to our corporeal being; the body as an incorporation of awareness and attention is also the invisible medium of experience. Strictly speaking, however, it is neither identical to a transcendental ego in Edmund Husserl's sense, nor to a "pre-reflective cogito", in the sense of Merleau-Ponty (at least, not if it is guided by the subjective sense of the word). It is – so to speak – mere anonymity, a language-game-shaped, "incorporated transcendence", i.e., *"condescendence"*, the point of intersection between immanence and transcendence. Hence, we have to speak about our body in another sense, too, namely as *"corporeality"*. This is the body in the double capacity of "sense-machine", "a spiritual automaton" in the words of both Spinoza and Leibniz, a "tode-ti" inside the event, and our very own otherness; *and* it is the trans-material, non-substantial substance which is able to melt together with the event. The body as mind, the *body-mind*, tries to circumscribe the event, and the event tries to invade the body-mind while at the same time processing and freezing sense. The body as the acting thing, as that which is able to co-merge with matter, is a living thing belonging to us, but also experienced by us, as something different from us, who are the hostages of the event. Hence, through the door between the alma-event and the proto-event we are let by the body into our corporeal activeness, and in this capacity, as spiritual automata, we meet the other zones of the event:

The tode-ti: Aristotle's concept of the singular object, the "haecceitas" by Duns Scotus, is the "facticity" of the material sphere, but this "facticity" is experienced as the meaning of the event as a link in the chains of causality, the "sunektikon aition" or "series causarum" in the vocabulary of the Stoic philosopher Chrysippos. This mode of experience denotes the presentation of relations and processes as if they were causally connected things. Thus the tóde-ti expresses a form of experience, both the beginning of the experience of the event as a pre-personal/post-personal, semantic entity, because the event begins to become an identity by being experienced as "some-thing"; and it is the distinct phenomena appearing inside the event as a carrier of sense. The "tóde ti", in the young Aristotle, is that which cannot be predicated of anything else, and hence, that which is immune to a final predication. It is the basic ontological and logic of matter, that which cannot be reduced to anything else. We can use this concept to designate the uniqueness of the event, and the uniqueness of its phenomena. However, when the sense of the event is raised to the level of the proto-event in the capacity of *"This happened"*, then the uniqueness is destroyed, because its spontaneity disappears, and the network of sense absorbs it, while the alma-event is slowly opening its abyss beneath sense – in the beginning just by letting us be aware of the general, non-unique, character of predicates, and later by discovering the contingency of predication.

The plasticity: the zone of the still indiscernible. It is constantly reproduced in the shape of the relation between figure and background, as a blurred "event-horizon". It is the oscillation between the known and the unidentifiable, a movement conducted by the word, and by the word as something older, wiser, and richer than the concept. This transcendence of sense is experienced as signification.

So there must be a kind of passage, a gliding, from the "tóde-ti", into sense-usurpation, which cannot itself as a process be the subject of sense, but transcends as an experience of a surplus of meaning, and as significance. In the language of Husserl, this passage cannot be an "intentional subject". The tóde-ti passes into a constellation, but during this process there is a constant tension in relation to the zone of plasticity, because the pragmatic-semantic destruction of the tode-ti, the "anascheuazein" is met by its seeking safety in significance.

At the level of this pre-conceptual passage the virtual and the actual are almost identical, to use the language of Whitehead and Deleuze, i.e. there is a vast set of possible worlds into which the "tóde ti" seems to be able to be inscribed as its proper sense ("It is the virtual that is distinct from the actual, but a virtual that is no longer chaotic, that has become consistent or real on the plane of immanence that wrests it from the chaos -..." What is ph. p. 156).

It is the right way to describe the tóde ti and the plasticity as simultaneous processes, because the experience of this-ness always creates a new background of plasticity and hence of ambiguity.

This tension between ambiguity and a secret meaning hidden as significance is always experienced in the dialogue as event. In particular, the dialogue as a subject of sense hovers in this equivocation. It is the task of the protreptic guide to keep it in this fruitful, but also frightening dizziness, until its genuine contours emerge by themselves from the interstices between the interlocutors. If the dialogue is successful, a new event is born in the event of dialogue, the event of mutuality. Only the emptiness of the alma-event makes this new sense-ascription possible.

The space/place: This zone consists of the permanent tension between the space, *chora*, as something constituting the content of experience, the lines of movement, the possibilities of being, but which remains a container and a background; and the *topos*, as the identified place, the familiar, that which we must leave all the time in order to become the ones who we probably could become. The tension of the ethos of the event is allocated here, because "ethos" also means the place of origin, which we, in the form of values, intentions, passions, and dreams, and in our character, are carrying with us all the time. In the protreptic dialogue there must be a movement towards that which is taking place as a sense for the chora, the real context as the common ground.

The Other person: the other individuals can be seen as possible worlds meeting us in the arena of the event, in which each individuals' corporeal being presents a secret to us – coming from his body, from his transcendental immanence, through his unique transformation into an epiphany of expressions, of cultural and historical otherness. The other person is "evented" by the words of the protreptic guide, and the protreptic guide is embodied by the immediate, an irreducible presence of a profound otherness.

The five elements of the event can be said to form a constellation at any point of time in the development of the event, and at any point in time form its interpretation in further events.

Perhaps it is already visible why this apparatus of analytical concepts created to grasp the event is needed to understand the protreptic dialogue? The point is that the proto-event is the level of psychological projections and strategic actions barring the virtual event from becoming actual between us. Thus, there must be a core of every event, a bottom, at which, sense can be destroyed in order to be built up anew.

The power of language games and games of truth must be able to be transparent on a background of positive non-sense. Also our motives, desires and games of power must vanish here too. However, passion must stay and increase. What must be sought for is the passion of reflection.

That the Stoics place "lekton", the exchange of sense, in the middle of the communicative event is of enormous importance. From this, one could conclude that a statement produced nearer the periphery would change the balance of the power of naming in a negative way. Involvement through "agape" has to have its costs, and power operates at the periphery. Modern theorists like Martin Buber, Gabriel Marcel, Emmanuel Lévinas, and Karl Rogers explore the inter-relational potentials of this middle (mesotes) at a level of positive, un-encroaching empathy, sympathy and insight into the other person which presupposes Christian altruism, Jewish Kabbalah, and democratic development, conditions which the Stoics, for historical reasons of course, could not match. But the more survival-centred focus of Stoic philosophy, during the chaotic times of Hellenism and the Roman Empire and its deism or even pantheism, blocked the development of an idealistic attitude towards communication, in spite of their theories of the social virtues ("oikeiosis" is the maxim of the well-guided duty-bound life, with the minimum-virtue "katechon", "officium"). The doctrine of "epimeleia heautou", the "cura sui", often comes too close to the "sui conservandi" which was shaped in its blunt objective form by Thomas Hobbes, and in its ideological form by utilitarianism and neoclassical economics in the form of the "enlightened self-interest" of the rational agent. Until the middle ages, during the great migrations in which Rome was destructed, Christianity had to fight both with itself and with eastern mysticism, Neo-Platonism, Gnosticism, and the proto-therapeutic Greek philosophies like Stoicism, Epicureanism, and the Cynic School, during its creation of a new institutional humanism. We know that this Christian humanism was eventually destroyed by intra-institutional decline until the Reformation, when altruism became a movement reaching into the people, in particular in the protestant sects, and hence, among the commons.

The renaissance of altruism was philosophically re-established by the Scottish (I think both were actually Scots!) empiricists like David Hume and Adam Smith through a secular concept of mutual benevolence, legitimated by its utility for both the individual and the community; and mutual understanding became a part of bourgeois ideology until the concept of solidarity in the working class overshadowed it as a global perspective – the bourgeois and Christian philosopher David Carlyle defended slavery as late as the last decades of the nineteenth century – and it was institutionalized in the welfare state. However, racism is still very much alive.

Our experiences with open communication and with an increasing focus on dialogue in organisations, nations and at the global, political level create another platform for thinking the other person – although it has its economic and technological reasons too, the concept of diversity management betrays them.

14.

Pragma and tynchanon

Now, there are two dimensions in the event. The first one is incorporeal, the other is corporeal. The idea was founded by Stoic philosophy in which one distinguished the "corporealia", i.e., the body, the material world, imagination, thought, and speech, from the incorporeal, the empty space, the void, time *and sense*.

The Stoics named the material dimension as a sum of processes, "the corporealia", *tynchanon*; and they named the incorporeal realm, "the incorporealia", the *pragma*, a level of being which encompassed that of sense, and transcended the personal, mental world of experience caught in the "phantasmata", the images of perception and thought. "Tynchanon" also means "object" in the Greek, but in this context of the event, it means the level of causes, whether they are conceived of as a chaos, or as a more mechanistic, causal flow. "Pragma", as already mentioned, has many important senses in the Greek. It generally means "act", "action", or "object", but in the "Poetics" of Aristotle it also means "action", i.e. "plot", and "sense". The Stoics used it to denote the phenomenon of "the sense of the event", hiding the "event of sense" and they are mutually understood as the immateriality of communication, the "lekton". Seen on the background of modern linguistic philosophy, in particular the formal pragmatics of speech acts, the Stoics appear amazingly insightful. This does not make them into dogmatically true protagonists of the right thinking, because their theory of both semantics and of the event has its limitations. However, the "lekton" expresses a very refined sense of the problems connected with the tension between mind and matter, and between determinism and free will, even if they could not epistemologically follow the problems as far as we are able to. The influence of the Stoics on Western thought become considerable during the Baroque, and from Leibniz and Spinoza to Foucault and Deleuze philosophers were heavily influenced by them.

It is important that the Stoics did not think of any causal relation between the tynchanon and the pragma as these cannot be ascribed any causal theory of meaning. The Stoics thought that the two dimensions coexisted, both expressing the cosmic logos. It was the ethical task of any individual to unite them, and this was the core of their ethos of the event, because the tynchanon followed the *"synektion aition"*, or *"series causarum"* – as Chrysippos named it –both the necessary and sufficient level of causes, the "iron hard laws of fate". However, the Stoics in general did not subscribe to any determinism, they only accepted fate (*heimarmene, fatum*), and this means that the attitude of the individual could be reconciled with a concept of personal freedom. The pike of this freedom was the ability to "prove worthy of the event" by meeting everything which happened with exactly the same mental attitude, the *"eudymia"*, the happy and calm assent to what might turn out to be even our own destruction.

One could claim that they saw rather an ethical difference between pragma and tynchanon than an epistemological and ontological one. This means that the Stoic wise could and should manage to live the distinctions between them, i.e. to defy merciless matter by the hand of sense.

It is no accident, of course, that Deleuze is so focused on Chrysippos in "The Logic of Sense"– the concept of dividing the work into "series" is probably a repetition of the way Chrysippos divided his enormous opus, of which nothing is preserved, alas.

Now, the problem is that mirrored from the level of the tynchanon, the world of distinct phenomena, the tóde ti, seems to have a rather firm identity– applying the concepts of causality and law both implicates and demands that. But in the capacity of pragma the range of its possible articulations seems rather wide. The pragma and the tynchanon present parallel lines which only seem to be able to meet when the tóde-ti crashes.

This was the way in which Heidegger in "Sein und Zeit" interpreted the Stoic concept of "procheiron", "Zuhandenheit": It jumps into reflection when action fails.

This figure of their possible interrelation reproduces the problem of Leibniz, manifested in the principle of the so-called "pre-established harmony", because it is impossible to point to a direct causal relation between tynchanon and pragma, even if there must exist some kind of powerful limitation arising from tynchanon. There must be some pre-structured direction of these rails for sense-construction, even if the material dimension cannot be grasped as something which automatically transforms itself into sense, i.e., into language games, or into attitudes or configuration of the will. So, if the event is conceived solely at the pragma-level – which Deleuze is inclined to do ("The event is sense itself, insofar as it is disengaged or distinguished from the states of affairs which produce it and in which it is actualised." The Logic of Sense" p.210, here Deleuze falls back on the theory of Bergson that sense-reception through the application of memory is unspatialized) – one reproduces the monadology of Leibniz. This line of thinking would by analogy conceive of the event as an immaterial entity without spatial extension, only defined by its properties, appetites, and cognitive program – this inevitably produces an aporia since the quality and intensity of properties, appetites, and thoughts presuppose space. In every monad, each state is the consequence of its former states, and it only relates to the realm of other monads through a more or less distinct perception of them. The pre-established harmony means that each monad reacts in the way it ought to react if there had been a real, materially mediated causality among them. Invested with a teleological perspective, and claiming the existence of an overall human capacity to reflect beyond monadic borders by creating a mega-synthesis, which Leibniz reserved for God, this thinking comes close to the idealism of Hegel.

The problem here could also be posed as the need to evade any kind of "symptomatology". This is only possible if we accept the pragma-level, the level of sense, and the definite predication of the event, as constitutive and effectuating in itself (as causa sui), i.e., as having causal power in relation to the level of tynchanon. This would not presuppose the vision of Prospero, that life is nothing but a dream, but instead poses the problem of that which Aristotle in the "Nicomachean Ethics" named *"deinótes"*, the force which transfers thought into action, theory into practice. The level of sense must be able to influence the level of the material. But the opposite must also be the case, even if we deny any direct causality.

This means that we have a very complicated structure of reciprocal causation here at the heart of the event. So we also have to accept some kind of causality, and hence, a contra-finality of Otherness, of the unfamiliar and almost anti-human level of the series causarum; and we have to accept an element of sense-creation too. This paradox can only be solved in accordance with the concept of "the subject of knowledge" with which we operate, and through the principle of translocutionarity. Bergson, Whitehead and Deleuze all chose, as I read them, to solve this problem by a rather drastic postulate about the material character of all phenomena C.S. Peirce chose precisely the opposite stance. The relation between matter and sense can then be solved through a postulate of levels of minute particles and their dynamic movements which at some point emerges into a level of phenomenal perception answering to the level of identified inner emotions, urges and images; answering to the level of objects which are big enough to be perceived and handled as objects by our body; and answering to elements of language. In my opinion the combination of evolutionary figures of thought and of vitalism does not explain anything at all, in particular not the reality of mind as a subjective experience, it only describes it from another meta-angle. It is after all this experience of mindfulness which makes sense and the social possible as phenomena.

Translocutionarity explains how mind as the sphere of autonomous incorporeality is transformed into the material sphere by the fact that voice is corporeal and hence, is able to causally influence other material beings, like human bodies. The material voice is in their sense-apparatus transformed into the incorporeality of sense and is thus able to influence their acting. The effect of physical gestures can be explained in the same way.

For protreptic it poses the problem of finding the principles and organic functions of sense-production between the two interlocutors. This does not imply a psychology of symptoms; quite the contrary. Causes must not be sought after rather, the mode in which sense becomes. Often this mode will reveal itself though the significance of what the other person says. Why and how does he speak as he speaks? The "why" must focus on the event: What does he want from the event of dialogue? This might reveal his habitual attitudes towards others, but also towards himself. His strategies of escaping the confrontation with his own values have great informational impact and could be said to reveal his particular fate (and hence the cruelty of tynchanon), of his memories and desires at the level of pragma ("April is the cruellest month, breeding Lilacs out of the dead land, mixing Memory and desire, stirring Dull roots with spring rain" as T.S. Eliot wrote). And indeed, the protreptic guide must both be a general, helping the other person to transform himself into a reflective anabasis (a military campaign into one's own country) into his own mind, and as a generous interpreter of this lyric be a poet himself.

15.

Protreptic and the symmetric event and the event of symmetry

The ethical principle of protreptic in relation to the event was expressed beautifully by Deleuze:

"Either ethics makes no sense at all, or this is what it means and has nothing else to say: not to be unworthy of what happens to you." (Log.d.s. p. 149)

But to be worthy of what happens to you is to be equal to the event, not just by enduring it, but by being its motor of transformation. To lead a dialogue is to make it worthy of what could happen to it. However, if not to be unworthy of what happens to you points at – what could be called – "the aesthetics" of the event, this would exclude the ethical perspective. Worthiness then means to carry pain and even destruction with equanimity, but what should one do with the pain of the other person? The strong soul will starve for its engagement – as Nietzsche put it – but how does the strong soul help other people, when the heroic gesture must be made in the hardly visible and often unsuccessful actions of everyday life? The tough and depressing practice of down to earth political life lacks drama and often ends in compromise, and in trivial everyday life so much happens which is not worthy of the label "event".

Deleuze's maxim here could be applied to Hitler's suicide, and it might well be interpreted as a legitimization of his act. For which reason, one must ask, is it more consequential for his life (or more in line with his life?), if he had chosen to meet his trial and death sentence? He did not seem to accept the law through which he would be sentenced? And what do we do with all the people who had to die in Berlin in the last months of the war due to his aesthetic self-relation?

Such an example shows that we cannot make an ethics on the basis of subjective capacities to receive the event, or on subjective consequence between life and acts, we must have both a normative perspective based on values, and knowledge of how these values are realized.

As already mentioned an ethics must also be sustainable at a level with no "eventum tantums" (great events), and even if this cannot be done through commandments, maxims and rules, there must be guidelines, or at least examples, and normative analyses of mental states, which can assist concrete decision.

Any sustainable ethics has concepts of creating symmetry between people.

The concept of symmetry is a Columbus egg. There cannot, given that we always exist in an event, be found any symmetry in the exact sense, because this would mean that the sum of knowledge, the sum of experiences, and the way they were formed (i.e. the individual epic and the theatre of memory, the communicative power, the empathic force, and the relation to values), were balanced precisely between two people. Sameness of age, gender, education, and hypothetical identity of experiences, even the twin-relation of genes, could not accomplish this. Neither could it be realized by Siamese twins, as long as the one Siamese twin had looked more on the other's face than on his own.

So symmetry must be produced from an original asymmetry in the event of dialogue.

The first rule to establish symmetry could be taken from Yamamoto Tsunetomo's records in "Hagakure", from "The Book of the Samurai", dating from around 1700. In this, he expresses in a clear and keen way some basic principles shared by protreptic:

"To a Samurai one single word is significant, wherever he must be. Through one word only he is able to manifest his fighting spirit. In peaceful times the word reveals the braveness of a human being, and in difficult circumstances one also knows that its force or cowardice could be experienced through one single word. This single word is the flower of the heart. It is not just something said with the mouth."

This testifies to aspects of symmetrical behavior, to equanimity and to the capacity to treat everybody with the same respect – this does not mean to treat them alike. Heidegger echoed this expression when he said that language is the flower of the mouth in his collection of essays on the philosophy of language, *Unterwegs zur Sprache*.

Yamamoto Tsunetomos states the second aspect mentioned:

"One must only speak in relation to the way in which one judges the emotions of the other person who is listening."

That is why the proptreptic guide must stay an anonymous human being but incorporate this being in expressing his own thoughts and feelings, when needed, in order to prevent the other person feeling naked. As attitudes towards the event, the principles of anonymity could be called "hetero-entic", based on the neologism "heteroenticity", remembering that "hetero" means "other", or "the other" in Greek. Heteroenticity should be seen as the opposite of authenticity (built on "auto" "self", or "auth'" "genuine") by focusing on the event and on the other person as that with which one must try to identify, where authenticity focuses on the capacity to prove similar to oneself in self-reflection and towards others, mostly for one's own sake – the last behavior is often called personal integrity, when it succeeds.

The concept of "authenticity" is classical Greek. It means to be genuine or to have absolute power. "Auth" means "genuine". It is the capacity to preserve oneself in any event by self-control, self-possession, self-confidence, integrity, and self-creation. While "heteroenticity" means to let the event be fulfilled through oneself, by becoming, by being generous, by liberating an inner force, and by compassion and we-creation.

Since Martin Heidegger's book *Sein und Zeit* from 1927 the concept of "the Existentials" has defined and dominated the way to be authentic in philosophy. These existentials are categories of existence focused on the subject, even if this subject is not identified with the ego, but with a more undifferentiated "being-there" a "being presented" by being. This mode of existence is characterized by understanding, insight, empathy, decisiveness, trust, goal-directedness, by knowledge of being "evented" or "thrownness", and by a general care about one's own existence. The existentials also allow for the insight into non-authentic ways of being.

The existentials strike the mode of being in relation to the event, but they are still in many ways indebted to the transcendental ego of Edmund Husserl. So we could contrast them with – what could be named – "Eventuals" from "eventum" in Latin, and hereby suggest modes of being much more focused on the interstices between human beings in the event in the capacity of the real subject of becoming. The eventuals emphasize the inter-relational character of being, the "de-centeredness", and the deep compassion manifested in normative actions through decency, seriousness, generosity, attentiveness, and a cautious incentive to shape the event and the other person.

Six eventuals can be discerned

1. Heterotelos

The goal of protreptic is Otherness. This could be named by the neologism "heterotelos", ("the Other person as goal") in order to give it a name in Greek, hereby shaping a terminology.

This first eventual expresses an attitude, which is carried by the knowledge, that we are constantly recreated by the event. To admit indebtedness to the event means to recognize all the way down the dependence on other people. This dependence can be seen as positive, as long as we are able to distinguish between that which is in our power, and that which is not – as most of the Hellenistic philosophies phrased it. To acknowledge the dependence on other people means to act as a non-servile servant of the other person. The protreptic guide is a servant indeed, and he is the "priest" of the event, producing its rituals and ceremonial spontaneously in the very process. He knows that the event is an empty place, and that the void and the whiteness of it must be met by the sound of understanding and the colors of compassion. If he preaches anything, it is the prayer of that which Plato and Socrates called "euprattein", the will and capacity to shape one's life in the image of the good. The interlocutors must "be happened" by the good, doing the good for the good's own sake, and finishing the event as a monument of the victory of the self over itself. The protreptic guide must *be* the event, and serve a beauty, which only appears when the sum of pain in the event is reduced by the realization of the potentials of pleasure to become. The basic feelings related to this eventual are wonder and awe, a utopian desire, and the belief in the impossible.

2. Synkatathesis

The second eventual is called *"synkatathesis"*, which in the Stoic terminology means to affirm in freedom, and affirming both the meaning expressed in the dialogue, and the autonomy of the interlocutors. The sense of the event is anticipated through an event of sense which is felt as a gift-box, which must be opened. The other person is the content of this gift, and his individual experiences are prerogatives which must be carefully interpreted, and developed. The memories, hopes, and dreams of the other must be fulfilled in the shape of precious value-goals, which have guided the other person's life and determined his career. Here the protreptic guide must distinguish carefully between the person and the human being, trying to encourage an identity which the individual hardly dares think of. The basic feelings related to this eventual are sincerity and love.

3. Lepsis

The third eventual is called "lepsis", an accepting and tender will to co-shape. The word "lepsis" means "reception" and also "well-coming" in the Greek. By this attitude a social space is opened between the interlocutors, and the inner constellation of the other person is accepted as an ultimate reality, which the two must investigate together. Here a free force is working in the event letting release and freedom happen. The protreptic guide must be the hostage and the witness of the "Third I" of the other person, and his life must meet an unconditional welcome. The basic feelings are solidarity, loyalty and hospitality.

4. Katafygé

The fourth eventual "katafygé", means "refuge" or "stronghold". The protreptic guide must be able never to judge, but on the other hand not to encourage to confessions, because what must be the

subject of the confessed are the values, not the person. In this aspect of the dialogical event a safe conduct must be granted, and
everybody is admitted into paradise. The basic feeling is compassion and unconditional acceptance.

5. *Prosoché*

"Prosoché" means "attention" in the Greek. The protreptic guide
must master the "hexis" of attentiveness, the self-shaping of an
increasing capacity to understand the spaces in the speech without anticipating. It needs a long training in self-awareness, the
awareness of the other person, the awareness of what takes-place,
and the awareness of one's own awareness. The basic feelings are
presence, sympathy, empathy, encouragement, inspiration, and the
kindness of intuition

6. *Ergon*

"Ergon" means that which is effectuated, the work. As such the
protreptic guide is a sculptor creating the event by removing the
superfluous marble. What must be uncovered is the contour of
the "Third I", the point of balance between internal and external
forces, the result of which is the perfect form. This sixth eventual contains the will to borrow power ("kydos" in Homér), to
become an anonymous part of that process of the event, which
is dedicated to normative consummation. The communicative
power of the protreptic guide is transformed from a privilege
into a task and into an obligation to surpass himself in receiving the other and the event as belonging to him. It is the will to
overcome oneself by accepting the victory of the event on its
behalf. The basic feelings are courage, the spirit of self-sacrifice,
self-conquest, and unselfishness.

The ethos of the event inherent in the eventuals is the capacity
to

Prove worthy of the event
To guide the secret of the event
To make the world ready for the event

As just stated the first principle cannot stand alone, it has to be
followed by a principle of carefulness towards the event which shall

always be a care for the secret life and suffering of the other person. But we also need a vision of the social, a utopia of the right events.

The presentation of the eventuals should show the attitude through which the symmetry in the protreptic dialogue is produced. The protreptic guide must be a mirror of the other person, he must guard his face by showing his own, and he must reveal himself through his voice.

16.

Rhetoric and protreptic

"Rhetoric is a counterpart of Dialectic;"

Such are the first lines of the fabulous "Techne rhetorike" by Aristotle.

"Rhetoric then may be defined as the faculty of discovering the possible means of persuasion in reference to any subject whatever." (I, ii, 1, The Loeb Edition).

Rhetoric works through proofs ("pisteon"). They are of three kinds:

"The first depends upon the moral character of the speaker (ethoi tu legóntos), the second upon putting the hearer into a certain frame of mind (akroatén diatheinei pós), the third upon the speech itself, insofar as it proves or seems to prove (auto to logo, dia tu deiknynai hé phainesthei deiknynai)." (I, ii, 3)

Of the three means to convince, "moral character, so to say, constitutes the most effective means of proof." (I, ii, 4-5). This statement does of course immediately free rhetoric from any accusations of being a means to strategic manipulations of other persons through persuasion. It is worth noting that there are several concepts of "attitude" or "mindset" in the Greek philosophical schools. Plato and in particular Aristotle who based his ethics on these concepts, would most often prefer *hexis* or *ethos* to *diathesis* when the issue is the strength of character, and the ethical and moral development of oneself. When "diathenein" is used in the above quote it means that it denotes attitude as such.

Hexis is translated by Cicero into "habitus", and from here

it passes into English as "habit". But the involuntary automatic connotations of habit are far from the sense of hexis.

Hexis is often used as a terminus technicus synonymous with *ethos* in Plato and Aristotle. The words, and in particular hexis almost as an onomatopoietic reinforcement, denote a spiral-like development-process, in which lies the vicious circle of needing theoretical knowledge of the good in order to practice it and only be able to know at this level by the experiences of practicing the good.

Ethos originates in two forms, one with an eta and one with an epsilon. The former denotes – so to speak – genetic basis *and* the shaping of this biological fundament of character through the habitat, the place of origin, and hence the transference of basic values through our upbringing. The latter denotes the degree to which one has been able to use this fundament of one's nature, and the educational incentives, in nurturing moral and ethical virtues.

In the Stoics the analytical hierarchy of attitudes uses hexis differently, putting it between *skesis* and *diathesis* in the hierarchy in which the former denotes the attitude of the animal, and the latter the attitudes of the supreme wise man. *Hexis* then refers to average social virtues.

Let us return to rhetoric.

There are three kinds ("genos") of speeches, depending on the situation and the hearers, the deliberative, the forensic, and the epideictic (symbouleutikón, dikanikón, epideiktikón). They refer to the future, the past, and the present, and they are all related to speeches in public institutions, mainly the political and the forensic, even if they can be used in a dialogue with only two persons (Rhet. I, iii).

These three modes of speech are also, and this is often forgotten, modes of listening too, even if Aristotle says, that these modes "correspond to three kinds of hearers" ("akroatai" in the Greek) – and please remember that "akróasis", "to be able to listen" – but also "to obey" – was a core virtue in the Stoic universe.

Any leader of private or public enterprises will use these three modes all the time and woven into each other. The deliberative mode is about giving advice. It deals with the future, with exhortation, and with prevention; "the end of the deliberative speaker is the expedient or harmful."[33] The forensic mode deals with the character of acts done, whether they can be justified or not; "The end of the forensic speaker is the just or the unjust." The epideictic mode deals with the norms or values of action; "The end of those who praise or blame is the honourable or disgraceful;"[34] In narrative all these modes constantly lead by turns.

To lead the event is to be able to receive the incident in the right way by creating the right moment through choosing the right mode, and hence, transforming the incidence into an event. Through these vertical level of modes of speaking and of listening the most powerful instruments of speech intersect, the example and the proof, the "paradeigma" and the "apodeixis", arguing through "the accepted beliefs".

In the case that employees question the reality and seriousness of the values of an enterprise, the leader might act as a protreptic guide and answer through the Platonic method of diairesis. He could choose to analyse these values critically, and to justify organisational behaviour, and chosen strategies – if they can safely be justified – through a logical deduction which testifies to the consistency and internal coherence of their interpretation. If he says that "we are a proper company" he could state the reasons for this by referring to the conceptual basis of decency. It originates in Aristotle' "Nicomachean ethics" in which "epieikeia", "fairness", and "prepon", "discrete decency", are core concepts. Cicero translates the former into "aequitas", "generosity" "equity", and the latter into "decorum", decency. "Equity" is an important concept in the Roman law meaning the duty of the judge to consider the conditions and context of the acts of the accused; while "decorum" means that this respect must be showed with careful discretion.

The leader might then argue that to be fair, proper, and generous the employee must be very careful in dealing with customers, first and foremost showing empathy and respect. This, however, can only be obtained when the employees develop a code of conduct towards each other based on the same principles.

"Here management must go in front", the leader could say,

---

33 Art of Rhet. I. iii, 5.
34 Ibid.

"and please do me the favour frankly of telling me when I did not match these criteria in my behaviour towards you."

But he might also answer with either a fictive example, or with a narrative from the firm's past which must not be questionable. Of course, he could involve himself in dialogues challenging the employees to try to substitute their own values as the basis of decency, but ethically this is a more risky business. If managers should try to do protreptic at all they must be able to take sides with the other person and sincerely relate to the values of the employee, and this could often be difficult unless the culture of the organization is tuned to criticism and is able to tolerate different personal attitudes.

In the end, the basic values of decency are justness and goodness.

However, if the leader should propagate organisational values in a protreptic dialogue it is utterly necessary that he is able to presuppose his own behaviour as the incarnation of these values, i.e., through the fundamental capacity which the Greeks named "ethos", the moral integrity. Moral integrity is a silent answer to any question concerning the area of responsibility of firm behaviour. It refers to a lived practice of interpretation and of performance the consistency and value-adherence of which cannot be questioned. In this way it reminds us of the unique style which makes us able to distinguish the master musician, as a platform uniting the performance of structure and freedom.

To the modes of speech, and to the methods of speaking, there respond three substances or matters of speaking, the "logos", the pathos" and the "ethos". The logos relates to the matter of which is spoken. It designates the objective domain of causes and effects, of means and their techniques, of professional knowledge and know-how, but also the realm of functionalism and pragmatics, of goals and ends. Hence, its basic value is truth. The pathos designates the passion. It deals with the ability of the speaker to make the hearer take ownership of his conviction, of his attitudes, of his norms and values on alternatively to be more convinced of his own. The basic value here is justness. This is also the realm of seduction, and hence of totalitarianism, and of the micro-fascism of the obvious, but it is the domain of the capacity of personal authority, too, because one does not need to be allured by the promises of enthusiasm, and hence, to deposit one's freedom – as Immanuel Kant once put it. Finally there is the ethos, the moral integrity, the personal equity of the speaker, ascriptions, which compel us to believe in his words. The basic values are the good and the beautiful, since doing the good for the good's own sake is an aesthetic gesture.

We are reminded of an excerpt from the little poem by Lewis Thompson with some of the most beautiful lines ever written:

"Christ, supreme poet, lived truth so passionately that every gesture of his, at once pure Act and perfect Symbol, embodies the transcendent. 'To embody the transcendent is why we are here.'"

These three dimensions of speech form a three dimensional matrix. They also create the pragmatic basis of the leadership of the event. If the leader is able to harmonise the deliberative, the forensic, and the epideictic modes of speech; if he is able to use argument and example with due respect to the "kairos", to the right moment; and if he is able to unite logos, pathos and ethos; then, in letting being be, he can obtain excellence.

When Aristotle describes the deliberative mode of speaking, the mode related to counselling and consulting, he actually uses "protrepon", "giving advice" or "exhortating".[35] "The "protrepon" in this context relates to the future, whilst the forensic mode relates to the past, and the epideictic mode relates to the present.

The "protreptikos logos" is also very important, because it pertains to the role of philosophy in society. This role is to give the ruler advice. In Plato, in the great dialogue, *The Republic*, there is a concept that distinguishes the leader: "euboulia", "to be well advised". The leader is well advised who is able to receive protreptic guidance, to let himself be exhorted by some chosen persons – I hope not by smart spin doctors – and at the same time by that which happens to him, and by his own experience. Two issues of learning really matter to the ruler. Isocrates, probably the most

---

35 Art of Rhet. 1358b, I, iii, 4-6.

famous rhetor of classical Greek – or better, speech writer, since he did not perform the speeches himself due to timidity and lack of voice – stated them: to be able to learn from his experience, and from history, on the one hand, and from norms or values, on the other. Cicero used to say that more rulers of city states appeared from the school of Isocrates than Greeks from the Trojan horse. And for sure, even Aristotle boasted about the rulers which he had advised. It was his luck that he did not live long enough to experience the full "success" of his most famous pupil, a certain Alexander, although Alexander only died one year after Aristotle.

The protreptic dialogue and its attitudes are the real basic condition of the above mentioned type of arguments and of the type of speeches, and like rhetoric it is subject to the same overall goal:

> *"Men individually and in common, nearly all have some aim, in the attainment of which they choose to avoid certain things. The aim, briefly stated, is happiness (eudaimonia) and its component parts."*

We can give a further specification of protreptic by stating that it is knowledge of how to direct speech in order to facilitate another person's recognition of the means to obtain happiness. Thus, as a type of rhetoric, it is without any intention directed at the consolidation of the power of the speaker in relation to the hearer. (Rhe. I, v). Its goal is to "inspire confidence in ourselves or others in regard to virtue." (I, ix). Thus, the one leading the protreptic dialogue is also meant to profit morally from it.

An aspect which protreptic shares with rhetoric is the communicative strategy to transform a suggestion into praise (épainos), i.e., by exaggeration or amplification to strengthen with purpose the traces of virtuous qualities in the other.

> *"Praise and counsels have a common aspect; for what you might suggest in counseling becomes encomium by a change in the phrase. Accordingly, when we know what we ought to do and the qualities we ought to possess, we ought to make a change in the phrase and turn it, employing this knowledge as a suggestion." (I, ix, 36).*

Thus by anticipating the good motives which the other person might have, one obliges him to make them to be made manifest. This deliberate emphasis on the good values of the other person might be seen as strategic, and in Aristotle it also is, since he treats rhetoric as a means to persuade an assembly. In protreptic, it must always be meant seriously. The protreptic guide must find the core values which "normally" would base the self-understanding produced by the receiver. The performative acts in protreptic dialogue must be extremely well controlled by the guide.

"When you say that equal salaries are a wrong principle, is this due to your concept of the just?" "I should think so." "What do you mean by justice, then?" "I mean to yield according to capacity and to accept according to merit." "But can this be just, since people are differently talented?" "The are also differently engaged." "But is this not a relative concept of justice?" And so on.

Another strategy is to interpret the acts and ways of a person through morally admirable examples, or to "compare him with illustrious personages, for it affords ground for amplification and is noble, if he can be proved better than men of worth." (I, ix, 38-39).

The intention of protreptic is to guide a person to find the best in himself, and not to identify with reproachable motives, even where they might be found. This is a method to raise a person through his own feeling of the guilt at not trying seriously to be the one which he could become.

Blame (psógos) does not belong in the mouth of the protreptic speaker unless it is directed to the harm the other person has done to himself by not seeing what his real interests or real capacities are. The protreptic guide can only directly be a judge about the truth or relevance of the analysis of the sense of words and values, because he all the time must be judging the other person's honesty towards himself. But he can only perform such judgment through indirect methods, i.e. through questioning, through feigned misunderstood interpretations of the other person's words, or through counter examples ("If a man speaks like that, what would you think about him?"). It must be stated that feigned misunderstanding only relates to the common sense of concepts, not to the motives of the other. For example, when discussing the reliability of a manager, the protreptic guide can ask: "Then a manager must always tell the truth, if one should be reliable?" knowing full well that no manager can tell all that he knows to the employees in any situation.

Neither does any form of irony belong to the repertoire of the protreptic guide, unless it follows the same lines of reproaching the other person for not having realized what was in his power, and what was not ("Here you were really hard on yourself (?), or perhaps "here you really took yourself in hand!" But the last ironical statement – it is not a question in the proper sense of the word – is seldom acceptable in protreptic dialogue). As for self-irony and humor they are allowed in most circumstances when it does not hurt the other's feelings.

The analysis of the number of motives, their states of mind, and hence of one's own character, are important procedures of the protreptic process – Aristotle mentions these three dimensions of action in relation to his investigation of the "genos dikanikón", the forensic type of speech, of accusation and defense, in the "Art of Rhetoric":

> *"first, the nature and the number of the motives to act unjustly; secondly, what is the state of mind (diakeimenoi) of those who act; thirdly, the character and disposition of those who are exposed to injustice." (I, x, 2).*

Let us now look closer into the phenomenon of motives in order to discover how the protreptic guide should conceive of and relate to them.

17.

The nature of motives

Any attempt to understand one's self presupposes the capacity to identify important motives, i.e. their types and numbers. This is, however, a complicated process due to several circumstances.

First, it demands knowledge of motives. Aristotle says that motives are identified through the knowledge of virtues and vices. The latter are stereotypical pictures of value-based actions and their opposites. Hence, a person must ratify the social set of values in order to proceed like that. But motives are conjectures of other qualities too. They are also identified through an image of what it means to be a human being, they presuppose an anthropology – e.g. very often a picture of man as a type of animal dominated by qualities symbolically ascribed to the beasts, or a creature fundamentally different from the animal, i.e. primarily a spiritual being, or a composition of both. Further they are identified through philosophical models of the interplay between mind and body, such as they are manifested in the many, different psychological theories the vocabulary of which migrates into common place language, as did the scholastic theories of motives transferred and transformed into the psychology of the Baroque in *Les passions de l'âme* by René Descartes, the *Leviathan* of Thomas Hobbes, the *Ethica* of Baruch de Spinoza, and the *Theodicé* and the *Monadologie* by G.W. Leibniz.

Perhaps the latter by Leibniz is the most interesting in this connection because of his concept of "petites perceptions" defining non-conscious levels of perception and mental activity presupposed by the "apperception" as a conglomerate of petite perceptions that can be clearly and distinctly known. This is interesting to compare to the statement of Aristotle:

"Men act voluntarily when they know what they do (poiusin osa eidótes), and do not act under compulsion. What I have

> *done voluntarily (proeirumenoi) is not always done with pre-*
> *meditation (eidótes); but what is done with premeditation is*
> *always known to the agent, for no one is ignorant of what he*
> *does with a purpose." (Rhe. I, x, 3-4).*

This distinction between spontaneous and deliberate action is
certainly pertinent to forensics, but it is always of fundamental
importance to self-understanding. In the nineteenth century this
dominant influence of the court as a metaphor of the mind – still
so central in Kant's mental model – decreases in influence since the
so called "unconscious" grows into a realm of possible motives
beyond the practice of ascribing juridical or religious guilt.

Self-reflection since Schopenhauer, Eduard von Hartmann,
and Freud, begins to be dependent on a hermeneutic of the self in
which identification of personal structures of motives no longer are
prone to moral judgment only, but orientates itself to unfulfilled
projects of life guided by a "hegemonikon" (the Stoic concept for
the core of personality) manifesting a new concept of identity. As
Michel Foucault notices in his book *Discipline and Punish* the first
juridical verdict taking a person's confused, and hence not deliberate, state of mind into consideration, appeared in the beginning or
the nineteenth century.

The reconstruction of the palette of motives suggested by the
new therapies used by psychoanalysis do not fundamentally differ
from the ones presented to us by the Greeks since they comprise the
antagonism between passion and intellectual will, but they tend to
make the values of the virtues symptomatic, and thus suspicious,
especially underrating the Greek cardinal virtue of "sophrosyne",
"temperance" or "self-command" directed by reason.

Since the subject of proteptic is sophrosyne, and inasmuch as
this means that the Freudian dictum "Wo es war, soll ich werden"
cannot be reached from its perspective in any other way but through
premeditated and deliberate reflection itself, therapy is generally
no option for protreptic: there are no shortcuts to knowledge of
one self, but only the main road of patiently practiced reflection.
This means that reflection does not have to be an object of other
forces than its own, when it is worked at sincerely.

Thus, protreptic would advocate for the optimum knowledge of the "diakeimenai" of the "quality of the state of mind" behind acting which Aristotle speaks about, and which is sometimes named "tropos", the "mood" of the agent, a word related to the root of pro-treptic", "trephein" or "trophein". Self-reflection demands the ability to identify one's own state of mind.

Today one would say that the third rhetorical dimension of the understanding of one's own acts, the identification of one's own character, can no longer be reached through the classical, so meticulously elaborated picture of "person type" developed in philosophy, psychology, and literature since Aristotle's follower Theophrastus. It can only be approached through the personal narrative. But the narrative would still be a refined version of the caricature – in spite of every delicacy in presentation – naturalizing character as a patterned flow, or as the famous "red thread" of Epictetus, but nonetheless naturalizing it, even in the potentially liberating biographical-utopian projections, or "lines of flight", by Michael White and his followers.

Thus, protreptic seems rather conservative in keeping to the distinction between virtues and vices, and to their inherent, normative basis, and ignoring all the recent attempts to substitute diffuse pictures of a situated personality for responsibility. Thus the picture of motives which protreptic deals with would be termed "rational" in the way Aristotle does, which means that actions generally should not be legitimated through any reference to "chance" (tyché):

> *"In short, all things that men do of themselves either are, or seem, good or pleasant; and since men do voluntarily do what they do of themselves, and involuntarily what they do not, it follows that all that men do voluntarily will be either that which is or seems good, or that which is or seems pleasant." (Rhe. I, x, 18).*

The whole idea of protreptic is that anyone should be able to analyze his own acts from the perspective that he is able to know what he finds pleasant and good. If we want, we do not need to have any secrets from ourselves other than the ones produced by our ignorance of the consequences of our actions. This could be called a program of the possibility of transparent autonomy, and hence, of the capacity for anyone to have himself in his own power (ton ef' hemin), to be the master of himself.

The therapist would often object that the neurotic or borderline person cannot distinguish the feeling of pleasure properly, or that something inside him blocks this knowledge, and that he cannot approach its complicated logic through reason. But protreptic does not share this view. Seeing the event as the subject of everything, the neurotic is caught in an event-horizon which he would be able to analyze if he began by analyzing what pleasure and pain mean in general, and after this, what they mean to him.

If a manager involved in a protreptic session confesses that his behavior towards the employees has made it impossible for him to reach his goals and at the same time unpopular, it would be misleading to support him in "admitting" that he did that because he did not like himself. In this interpretation he should have known the exact consequences of his actions, and at a certain "motivational level" he should have either sought pain himself or to inflict that on others. It is far more likely to suppose that he did not understand the nature of action, of interrelations, and the minds of other people. He simply lacks knowledge of the social, and of himself.

But let us say that his results were brilliant concerning effectiveness, but that he had become disliked to a certain degree. This situation was, and still is, often seen. He could then claim that he does not care about the feelings of the employees towards him. The question is, whether this actually could be the case? The difference between most psychology and protreptic would here consist in the fact that psychology would not accept his claim, while protreptic, at least hypothetically, would. So, protreptic would neither postulate that he did not realize his own feelings, nor that he had ignored his real interests, but try to find the normative basis of his claim. The problem posed would then be: "What values and criteria direct this attitude towards others so that their opinion of you does not matter?"

As a starting point one cannot stipulate that such values do not exist. It might enhance pleasure to ignore the verdict of others in the short run. In the long run, however, it is impossible, because this would imply that one had chance in total command, being absolutely independent of the course of the events. However, this dilemma is more complicated than it might seem, on the one hand, because it dispenses with what it means to understand another person. If one feels that another person disgusts or loathes one, this would very often be experienced as an expression of hate. Hate could be explained as the result of one's action towards another person, but just as often, or actually, it is explained as a result of the character or of the "mental economy" of the latter. In both cases one is able to stigmatize him morally, and hence, remove the cause of his feelings from oneself. As far as one does not relate the hate to traits of one's own character, or to actions done, this hate can be a case for implementing values to one's own advantage, accusing the other of violating the moral rules among men (the concept of "projection" is not a proper approach to the autonomy of an acting person on the basis of values).

Another way to place the feelings of other's at an arm's length is to conflate them in a "they". "These" people do not want to work properly, "they" do not wish to yield to other rules than their own, etc.

Both strategies can be attacked by emphasizing that more than one or two people sharing the same feelings might betray that the one towards whom they have such feelings might be part of the cause. Sidestepping on the manager's behalf could imply his reference to group dynamics, to the evolution or emergence of collectively hostile attitudes without a significant cause, but in spite of all explanations he would still be left with the fact that he is disliked, and be asked to face his own attitude towards his ability to raise such feelings. He could be asked how he himself feels in the state of disgust or anger, and so be forced to confront the fact, that feeling anger also implies to suffer. Probably few people would claim that they enjoy their own feeling of hate, and if this is admitted by a person, he must also admit that he causes other people to suffer by making them hate him. And here he would not be allowed to answer that their hate would be their own fault, for he has already said that he fully knows that his way of acting is not popular.

Anyhow, it is not so difficult to nail him in a position where he is obliged to answer the question "Would you not prefer that the employees liked you?" Here we touch on the second aspect of the dilemma which is about the manager's knowledge of the nature of pleasure. On the one hand he has admitted that his behavior might reduce the pleasure of the others, and even inflict pain. On the other hand he is now confronted with what it means to ignore the pain of other people, and this displaces the value-problem inasmuch as he must compare the values connected to effectiveness with the values connected to personal relations.

Here he might answer that we are actually talking of two different ways of doing the good, but then he shall be caught in his own trap, because the protreptic guide can ask: "Who decides then what the good is in these two connections?" Whatever he might choose to answer he cannot escape confronting the fact that the good defined by effectiveness is a value represented by the most powerful stakeholders, the top management and the privileged shareholders. So the nature of the good would depend on whom one wants to please. Again, this leads us back to confront the fact that the role of recognition cannot be ignored generally, and that the ignorance of the recognition of one group is only possible because the recognition by another is earned thereby.

Through this procedure the one doing the protreptic has brought his interlocutor into a situation where he has to answer which values are basic to his concept of his own identity.

In connection with the subjects treated above, an immense problem presents itself as to the meta-language by which one describes oneself and other people.

Values are incorporated into action through desires, passions and reflective deliberations, through character and social roles, and hence we are not conscious of them *qua* values all the time.

This is one basis of what I would call the *epic language* of common sense.

This language can be performed at many levels, but let me quote from one of the most excellent examples, from some of Robert Musil's descriptions of characters and relations in his "The Man without Qualities" (the translations is mine).

Musil is describing a beautiful distinguished lady, Bonadea", who gives herself up to the principal character of the novel, Ulrich. She has betrayed her husband infinitely many times, however:

"The psychological effect produced by her for years having yielded to a human being, the wife of whom she had become more due to calculation than from the inclinations of the heart, had in her created the illusion that she by nature was unnaturally prone to catching fire, and this had made this fancy almost independent of her consciousness. An inner force which she could not understand fettered her to this man who was favored by circumstance; she despised him due to the weakness of her own will and felt weak in order to be able to despise him; she betrayed him in order to escape him, but simultaneously spoke, at the most improper moments about him or about the children whom she had with him, and she was never able to liberate herself totally from him" (Chapter 12).

Notice an expression like "she despised him due to the weakness of her own will and felt weak in order to be able to despise him." This is a description of unconscious motives, or motives in the interstice between conscious and not-conscious states of mind. Or perhaps it is a reconstruction of an actual, but not-conscious, state of mind by the description of conscious motives.

Is this a psychological description? To a certain degree, I should think so, insofar as it might fit some psychological theories of projection, common to many different schools of psychology. However this statement could be made by an uneducated farmer. So, we must ask, do psychological conceptualizations grow out from common sense experience, or vice versa? If Musil had used the concept "super ego" from Freud this would be clear enough, but this vocabulary of self-deception, after all could also be what characterizes literature, and hence epic language. It certainly belongs to an author who allows himself to describe his person's minds from within. But this could only be done through some collective ratified concepts of introspection.

The problem is to what degree protreptic is allowed such a language, because in the capacity of inductive generalization it might definitely be wrong.

Here comes another example from Ulrich's first visit to his friends the couple Walther and Clarissa. Walther is an unsuccessful, but gifted artist, who has been fluctuating between painting and playing. By the time of the visit he plays Wagner on the grand piano:

> *"'Frog-king!' she said and nodded behind her towards Walther or the music ... During his last visit she had told him about a terrible dream: A salacious creature had thrown itself over her while she slept; it was a soft-stomached, tender and horrible big frog and it was the symbol of Walter's music." (Chapter 14)*

Musil is a master of metaphor, but of course we all are through our dreams. A dream is, so to speak, a metaphor of metaphor. However, we are not told whether the connection between the dream and her husband Walther is the result of her own reasoning, or an interpretation by Ulrich.

Is protreptic allowed to use metaphors? Since so much of language has a forgotten metaphorical basis we are forced to apply them. The question is to what degree could we deliberately use metaphor as a subject of the dialogue and as a technique – well known from therapy?

I think that deliberately developed metaphors could be used in protreptic, but also that spontaneous metaphors of the receiver could be addressed, as also could dreams.

It is a problem whether the phrases of the first example are really metaphoric? Not exactly, I should think, although they might have been drawn from forgotten examples from myth and literature: The weak hero despising his opponent instead of respecting him, and emphasizing his own bad day as an opportunity misused by the opponent due to the lack of nobility.

Musil operates at a level referring to the interpretation of the behavior of others created through introspection, and through causal knowledge derived from observation. A further example invented here might make this clearer. I state about a person whom I know: "As a young man he did not care about working, he seemed to waste his time, but some day he got caught by this reality, and now it has for many years been like an obsession!"

As a prototype these personality traits were expressed by Falstaff about his King.

You might presume from this statement that I know such

radical change from myself, perhaps in a smaller dimension, or that I have observed it in somebody I know, or even that I have seen or read Shakespeare's play "Henry V".

We must now look at the semantic of this statement. It expresses a proper transformation, thus it presupposes two different stages of life. The first question would be whether the descriptions of these stages are probable? Let us accept that insofar as they are thinkable, however dependent on their internal and external causes. The external cause might be subsidies from a rich father, which suddenly disappear for whatever reasons, but "empirically" they seldom end up in happy obsession with work. A great love could be a cause of change, but this does not prove right, since this love should be the subject of obsession – and the influence of a woman has to be extraordinarily strong if such effects should result. However, a heavy responsibility put on his shoulders, and his discovering of its significance might be an external incentive, but after all this must in some sense have been prepared already from within.

So let us turn to internal reasons. One is inclined to claim that he "wakes up", that he finally had found his vocation. And this means that we presuppose that he had sought a goal, or had one already but sought its proper embodiment

The problem lies in the ascription of reasons. Is this drama actually to be seen at the level of values, or at the level of psychic, often more or less irrational or even non-discursive, forces?

At the meta-level it could also be discussed whether the transformation displays a causal relation between the two phases of his life, the weakness in the first period enforcing the strength in the following. But such causal connections arise from the application of values. After all, why should the meaning of the first phase be judged from the meaning of the last? And which criterion is at play here? Is it just a doctrine of the morals of work? If the second phase seems happy, so the first one might have been too, since they are both a certain modus vivendi?

Here it can easily be seen that protreptic presupposes a mental model and a rather virtuous overview of values and the relations connecting them. But at the same time the protreptic has to resist any suggestive explanation.

To the protreptic guide the dilemma would always be that as a human being he cannot help to think spontaneously in these ways, i.e. along common sense lines, but as an earnest facilitator he must believe in his own experience. This dilemma can never be solved, but it can be softened by a severe consciousness of any ever so tiny thought. The work on oneself, "askesis", is the basis of protreptic.

18.

The state of mind

Both the state of mind (diákeimai) and the character are of great importance to the success of the protreptic speaker as it is in all the three types of rhetorical speeches, because they influence the emotions of the hearer, and hence, "independently of demonstration … induce belief." (Rhe. II, I, 5).

The protreptic speaker must generally display good sense, virtue, and good will (phronesis, areté, eunoia). This is not because the protreptic speaker must convince or persuade; in this he is very different from the rhetoric speaker. The aspect of convincing is only related to the hearer's capacity and willingness to take his own life seriously. This is the only message.

The state of mind of the protreptic speaker must thus be shaped by earnest and sincere interest in the one to whom he is speaking. However, he must prove himself reliable by demonstrating good sense. This does not mean that he shall appear authoritative, but he must be trustworthy.

Since the protreptic dialogue is directed towards the realization of values, the protreptic guide must first and foremost have an intense contact with his own value basis, and further he must be very versed and versatile in both the abstract relations of values, and in the concrete consequences of them in relation to actions, emotions, and events. The latter means that he must be able to judge the relevance of the stories and episodes used by the answerer to illustrate the values treated.

But what is a value?
A value is a possible mode of certainty. This certainty cannot be grasped through a denotative relation between a discursive phrasing of it, most often called a "maxim", and a prescribed act, since there is no unambiguous state of things which would answer to it. Of course, normative propositions cannot be deictic

or denotative, since they describe prescriptive states of mind, but their resulting act can be compared with the iconic ideal of the maxim. The norm behind the maxim is not an icon, it comes closer to the modern conception of "symbol" (stemming from Goethe) as a sign pointing to a sense only accessible as significance, and never completely. Hence, a value, being a species of the norm cannot refer directly through representation, but only indirectly through discursive phrasing and through paradigm. It cannot be understood through what the Greeks called "bebaiótes", loosely invoking the representational truth structure of proposition, the "veritas adaequatio est rei et intellectus", but must respond to the concept of "aspháleia", the inner certainty born by a conviction of the possible state of things. As already put forward by Immanuel Kant, a maxim cannot be applied to the world through any further rules without implying an infinite regress, because one would have to have rules for the application of these rules, and so on.

So a value is a capacity, a way of the "I can". "Can" originates in O.E. 1st & 3rd pers. sing. pres. indic. of "cunnan", "know, have power to, be able," (also "to have carnal knowledge"), from P.Gmc. *kunnan "to be mentally able, to have learned" (cf. O.N. kenna "to know, make known," O.Fris. "kanna" "to recognize, admit," Ger. "kennen" "to know," Goth. "kannjan" "to make known"), from PIE base *gno-. Absorbing the third sense of "to know," that of "to know how to do something" (in addition to "to know as a fact" and "to be acquainted with" something or someone). Since all knowledge has a normative basis, in every ever-so-trivial practice, like combing one's hair, or cooking an egg, a value system is incorporated, which can be reconstructed in the form of an axiology. Socrates was right: All action depends on knowledge of the good – whether one acknowledges it or not – and the good must not be mistaken for the direct feeling of pleasure. A value is an "I can" based on knowledge, and a knowledge based on what we have done, and will be able to do, and guided by ethical imagination and by both deliberate and intuitive judgment. Since the word also means "to have power to", it resonates perfectly with the Greek ideal of knowing what is in our power.

We are embodied, always situated, value systems, based on

experience and memory, and incorporated in character. So a value can be defined as a *phronetic capacity*.

"Phronesis" is a key concept of Greek philosophy, and we shall return to it after a digression to the concept of "maxim".

Aristotle defined a maxim in his Rhetoric, II, xxi, 2, in Greek called "gnomologia", from "gnomé", a concept with many different senses: "capacity of knowledge", "reason" "sense", "insight" "conviction" judgment", intention", "decision", "will" "apophthegm" and "advise"; and "will", and "logos" thought" or "discursive phrasing"– but usually shortened to "gnomé"– as "a statement, not however concerning particulars…, but general; it does not even deal with all general things, as for instance that the straight is the opposite of the crooked, but with objects of human actions, and with what should be chosen or avoided in reference to them." Thus "maxims are the premises or conclusions of enthymemes without the syllogism." "Gnomon" is the origin of our word "norm", but in this book we distinguish between maxims and norms, where the latter cannot sufficiently be stated discursively, but are embodied as virtues too.

This means that maxims are statements which have an underlying enthymeme, knowledge not demanding apophantic knowledge, i.e., "conclusions should not be drawn from necessary premises alone, but also from those who are only true as a rule" (Rhe. II, xxii, 3). However, this also implies that such potential premises must not demand long chains of analytical reduction, neither as a tacit presupposition, "nor should it include all the steps of the argument." (Rhe. II, xxii, 2-3).

One example given by Aristotle is:

"No man who is sensible ought to have his children taught to be excessively clever".

This comes close to a proverb or a apophthegm, and it is obvious that such statements belong to the mores of a society, and that they are not necessarily ethical in their content.

It becomes an enthymeme if and when "the why and wherefore are added, for instance, for, not to speak of the charge of idleness brought against them, they earn jealous hostility from the gentiles".

This means that a maxim need not be proven by demonstrative proof, because it is evident due to common sense, or that it only needs such a one if it goes contrary to the general opinion. If the maxim needs a further premise or a conclusion, called an "epilogos", this could refer to something evident to common sense, and is apt to use, even if one knows that the premises are wrong ("for because they are common, they seem to be true." Rhe. II, xxi, 11). This is because rhetoric deals with the creation of conviction in certain situations, and in certain people.

Thus proverbs could also be used, and Aristotle sounds almost as manipulative as Hitler in "Mein Kampf", when he states:

> *"Further, maxims are of great assistance to speakers, first because of the vulgarity of the hearers, who are pleased if an orator, speaking generally, hits upon the opinions which they specially hold... Wherefore the speaker could endeavor to guess how his hearers formed their preconceived opinions and what they are, and then express himself in general terms in regard to them." (Rhe. II, xxi, 15).*

This, of course, cannot be tolerated in protreptic dialogue. Neither is the advice "to express in general terms what is not general in complaint or exaggeration" which Aristotle also suggests in the same context acceptable, but it is important to realize that protreptic dialogues must search for the general, but certainly without being manipulative.

For Aristotle, the greatest advantage of maxims is the use that would "make them ethical":

> *"Speeches have this character in which the moral purpose is clear. And this is the effect of all maxims, because he who employs them in general manner declares his moral preferences; if then the maxims are good, they show the speaker also to be a man of good character" (Rhe. II, xxi, 16).*

In protreptic the moral purpose must be clear, but maxims must never be used as means to admonish that the receiver ought to act in some way..

A value is always far more than a maxim. It is the mental environment in which the maxim makes sense. Through it, the dispositions, emotional atmosphere, and the relevant modes of reflection which they give rise to are conjured, and hence the possible ways of action are prescribed. Due to the uniqueness and complexity of any event, values must be the foci of attention, and hence, individual modes of guiding one's experience towards a goal set by a norm. A value is a set of criteria for distinguishing salient traits in the event, and a tacit capacity for acting this knowledge out guided by the image of the other person conveyed by benevolence. Feeling responsible towards another person limits the strategic use of psychological common sense knowledge often so brutal and cynical in its core.

The mental functioning of values are inextricably connected to two capacities philosophically related to the aesthetics of Immanuel Kant, the sense or capacity of judgment, and imagination or fantasy. The capacity of judgment appears where reason does not suffice, or a capacity used when the relevant or sufficient information is lacking. Fantasy is a type of event-sense making it feasible to realize a value in all situations. So it is legitimate to speak about "ethical fantasy".

The capacity of judgment is sometimes understood as an aspect of the Greek concept of *phronesis*. This concept is rather complicated, because it has several meta-levels in Aristotle, and because it was translated and transferred through different interpretations.

Phronesis is the core concept in the book on "Protreptic" by Aristotle. However, its modern interpretation is often very diffuse, because it is translated as "practical wisdom" and in Latin as "prudentia" and "sapientia", concepts also found in English. But phronesis is not just prudency, neither is it just sapience. The main problem arises because the Greek did not distinguish between theoretical and practical knowledge in the same way as we do. In Greek thought successful practice means a practice which is in harmony both with the state of the world in the event, and with the mind of the actor. However, harmony of mind is only possible on the basis of an ethical attitude. Practical wisdom does not mean empirical knowledge of men and their affairs, but knowledge of oneself. But knowledge of oneself is at the same time knowledge of the ethical norms and the capacity to realize them. This means that phronesis is incorporated in ethical virtues. No virtues can be realized without phronesis, but even if phronesis does not suppose apophantic knowledge, because it deals with the possible, not with the necessary, it presupposes intuitive knowledge, "nous", and a portion of genuine wisdom of the absolute, "sophia" or "gnosis".

It is often supposed that phronesis is identical to prudency, especially in much literature on management, but this is by far the case.[36] Prudence rests on a refinement of "doxa", of common sense, and might be "endoxa", "high-level-common-sense". Its focus is on cleverness and even cunning ("métis" or "deinótes" in "The Nicomachean Ethics") and hence might include the ethically insufficient way of acting. The knowledge of life which a person might pick up through active partition in a war might be very different from the knowledge he would pick up from the work in a high school, though it needs not be, if it concerns the basics of human behavior. Only if it emphasizes the human possibilities of self-forgetting and self-sacrifice, courage, solidarity and loyalty, it might exemplify phronesis, since phronesis differs from prudence while its goal is not to produce survival or acceptance of the status quo, but criticism, utopian vision, and a life based on radical normativity. We cannot, of course, simply accept the world view of the Greek aristocracy to whom Ulysses still hovers as an ideal image of the wise man we have to look at phronesis on the background of the development of Western humanism since the Renaissance. This does not mean, on the other hand, that we should accept the rather ridiculous or fantastic views launched naively by post-modernism relying on Nietzsche's tragic-comic attempt to revalue all values, nor on his epistemologically unfounded postulate of a consciousness without a self. Deconstructionism and constructivism are academic disciplines which acknowledge or bring to light some serious ontological and epistemological problems, but they try to "solve" them at a level far more feeble and self-contradictional than the traditional basis of these problems itself reveals. Philosophy week enough to be philosophy a la mode is dangerous and pathetic in its

---

36 See my article "Phronesis as the Sense of the Event." IJAR, 1/2009, Rainer Hampp Verlag p. 68-114.

vanity at the same time. The most blatant example of this nearly screwed idiot-savant-mode to practice philosophy is probably the work of Paul de Man.

The capacity to live for the virtues might to a certain degree be an inborn capacity; it belongs to the "aristos", to the gentleman of noble proper – this is certainly the view of Aristotle – and it is a product of the upbringing and lifelong learning (the paideia), but it is first and foremost a result of "askesis", of hard work to perfect oneself. So nobility has quite another sense to us, it means a quality which one grants oneself.

Phronesis is given to us through the way we act in the event. It is closely related to another cardinal value, to "sophrosyne", "temperance" and "self-control". It is the junction of our "êthos", of our constitutional character, and of our "ethos", our will and capacity to transform the given, normative values into action, and through this effort to create our character ("ethopoiesis"). The creation and development of phronesis is the goal of protreptic.

Phronesis is the event-sense, a normatively guided sense. It is the principle of self-reflection, and is directed towards the winning of the war against oneself – as Plato speaks of in the dialogue *The Laws*. Phronesis opens and guides the entrance to the self by mastering its becoming, and it produces the right feeling of self, "ho phronema". Thus phronesis exemplifies the movement denoted by the concept of "hexis", a self chosen, deliberate, action-directed "tropos", a state or disposition permanently created by an inner force. This is the way in which Aristotle argues in his "Nicomachean Ethics*".

Hence, phronesis manifests itself in an ethical fantasy in the event and directed towards the other person, but it is also a way to help oneself to the ideal of "ton ef' hemin", to master one's life. It implies a radical sense of possibilities, combining experience, and memory with thought. Phronesis is an individual strategy of "epimeleia heautou", of taking care of oneself, but it is both a meta-value at the highest level of the moral virtues, and a dianoetic, or intellectual virtue, being both a species of praxis and poiesis, and in the end contemplation – "theoria", "deep insight", with the mind-forming result of phronesis being translated in Latin into "contemplatio". Thus phronesis is always more than poiesis, being creation in relation to some external goal, while the genuine goal of phronesis is a practice in which the good is practiced for the sake of the good.

It is now the time to pose some principles of protreptic to make the different aspects presented here more palpable. Protreptic is a systematic method in the proper sense of the word, since it prescribes and excludes attitudes and practices, but it is also open to new knowledge and techniques, even if its axioms in relation to dialogues and its axiology are established.

19.

The principles of protreptic

The principles of protreptic can be listed thus:

The first principle
Protreptic must anchor the cognitive achievements appearing in the dialogue in a knowledge which transgresses experience. This principle is crucial since it challenges the traps of the rhetoric hidden in especially simplified narrative therapy and some schools of coaching. The character of this trap is very well phrased by Aristotle, when he states that the enthymemes of speech must neither presuppose long chains of reasoning, nor must they articulate the obvious discursively in the capacity of premises:

> *"It is this that makes the ignorant more persuasive than the educated in the presence of crowds; as the poets say "the ignorant are more skilled at speaking before a mob." For the educated use commonplaces and generalities, whereas the ignorant speak of what they know and of what more nearly concerns the audience." (II, xx,ii, 3).*

The danger of the narrative is that it is all too suggestive, almost all television and all pulps, but also the most serious epic and films pursue the story. We are certainly "in Geschichten verstrickt". This epitaph originates in the title of the book "In Geschichten verstrickt. Zum Sein von Mensch und Ding" – "Caught in stories. About the Being of Man and Thing", as the title of an important book by Wilhelm Schapp from 1953 sounds, a book trying to unite the life-world with history and escaping logocentrism. This is obviously the challenge to protreptic, not at least when it is practiced in groups, with or without an experienced facilitator, because the task is not only to be critical towards "what one thinks one knows", but to be able to rethink this apparent knowledge at a higher level of abstraction. The goal is not only to purify the concrete knowledge of its mounting in the situation and its contexts, in order to operate at a level of demonstrative knowledge – this often opens up another trap, the dogmatic-philosophical – but to make this knowledge more real, by screening its personal bias.

Particularly in groups, people are inclined to talk about personal events and to fall back on stories, thus mistaking examples for prototypes. Of course knowledge of human action must be vitalized by personal experience, but it must not be lost in these types of often anti-reflective illustrations that never even reach a proper level of interpretation, and definitely not the level of meta-interpretation searched for by protreptic.

Personally experienced events and personal narratives are a natural part of protreptic, but only against the background set by what must be really meant by abstraction, a conceptually enriched knowledge of what is talked about.

The second principle

Protreptic must establish criteria of truth for empirical knowledge and of the limits of such knowledge in relation to the capacity to understand oneself and another person. This is a very difficult venture, since we only know ourselves from our inner perceptions, of which we are the only receivers and witnesses. So the road to self deception lies wide open.

It is difficult to say in how many ways we are forced not to deceive ourselves. Probably the pragmatic perspective, the need for action in a shared reality, is the dominant reason, but there are others. If we had a kind of seismograph or barometer of pleasure and pain, their measurements might prompt us to stop self-deception where it already produces, or predicts, too much pain, even if its deliberate goal was pleasure. Also there might be a sort of "reality sense" in relation to one self – not the same as a "reality principle" from the Freudian terminology – which demands the Greek dogma of "epimeleia heautou", the taking care of oneself.

The famous Kantian questions: "Was kann ich wissen?", "Was soll ich tun?", "Was darf ich hoffen?" ("What can I know?", "What must I do?", "What shall I hope for?"), form the key subjects of his first, two major oeuvres, "Kritik der reinen Vernunft" and "Kritik der praktischen Vernunft". They are questions which anybody must be able to answer for himself in order to "stay real".

The third principle

Protreptic must establish personal laws for valid processes of thought.

This means that I must be able to learn to think by using the rules of common sense logic, but beyond this to establish my own points of contact with the truth. If these contacts are all too loose, I shall be trapped in phantasms, idealism, and a credulous attitude to common sense and to science. This will leave me without the necessary autonomy, and without the means to establish it. The capacity to think critically from my own point of view is the goal of protreptic. And this goes for both parties in the dialogue.

The fourth principle

Protreptic must establish a normative system, a system based in general values interpreted personally, and functioning through the elements of an axiology. Such an axiology is of a general character, but might be situated due to age, gender, social background and the setting of the event and its contextual framing.

One must create a normative system built on the four basic values of culture, the good, the true, the just, and the beautiful. When this is chosen in freedom, it will obligate the individual through the knowledge guided by reason to a normative acting, the principle of which is that it alone shall lead to individual and collective happiness.

Protreptic is meant to create an urge and a mode of experiencing and reflecting which furthers a permanent ethical development, facilitating the other person's re-foundation in his basic values, and creates a lifeline to the sustainable values of society. Protreptic should at its best inspire the other person to become the master of his own house by being able to control and direct his passions, and to look through his self-deceptive strategies. This demands an increased level of attention upon which must be worked hard, if it shall not disappear. As already stated several times it is about the capacity to distinguish between that which is in our power, and that which is not. The goal is to liberate oneself by acting for the sake of the good.

These principles can be gathered in a single one: *To learn to think in the right way.*

20.

The difference between protreptic and coaching and therapy

The most important difference between these three approaches to dialogue hold by therapy, coaching and protreptic is the ideal of symmetry peculiar to protreptic. The protreptic guide acts as real guide, he asks, suggests, and is not afraid of controlling the dialogue, even if he tries to let the other define the path until the moment has come, when it is time to confront the other with what he says or have said.

Further differences are that in protreptic existential questions are posed, like: "What is a life?", or "What do you want with your life?" These could be asked by therapists and coaches, but only deep into a conversation, and only on special occasions, if the question is prepared by the client or the coached. Also protreptic does not, as a matter of principle, try to identify a person psychologically, neither does it ascribe qualities, nor does it operate with psychological types of any kind. This is very different from therapy and coaching as far as their meta-theory is psychology. Of course it is often a program of good therapy and good coaching to suspend judgment in the beginning, and to resist projecting, but their frame of reference are models of personalities which rely on typologies. Even the contribution of C.G Jung with its important background in a Kantian version – what, in order, to hint at their metaphysical roots could be called a "psycho-cosmology" – uses rather crude distinctions from common sense like "introvert" and "extrovert" to design its types of character. Freud was certainly a great hermeneutic philosopher, but his material metaphysics in "Das Unbehagen in der Kultur" ("Civilization and its Discontents") is to my opinion not convincing. Another philosopher trying his hand on a material metaphysics almost at the same time, Alfred North Whitehead, is also caught in self-contradictions and falls victim too to the traps of over-systematization.

If protreptic has a program it is to suspect everything that appears obvious in explaining the other person, included the obviousness felt by the protreptic guide himself on the basis of intuition. Intuition is of course built on personal experience, but it is driven by common sense. The declared admiration of common sense stated by Bergson in "Matter and Memory" also forces him into incoherencies, and to the tacit negation of his own program, since he refers so much to neurology, and tries to transgress common sense carried introspection.

Even if an abundance of functional explanations of basic values like the good, the just, the true and the beautiful can be produced, protreptic would never use them. A basic value is a social and a mental fact in spite of its ambiguity, even if it may differ in accordance with history and culture.

Protreptic does not seek symptoms; it seeks problems of a normative kind attempting to reduce what the other says to his basic values. Thus the protreptic guide does not look for desires and their personal economy of fate, but looks for the values driving and legitimating desires.

Of course there are schools of therapy the principles of which come close to the ideals of protreptic, like the symmetric dialogue propagated by Carl Roger's client oriented therapy.[37] Rogers states among others the following principles: "... a concern with the philosophical and value issues that grow out of the practice of therapy." The point is to lay "a continuing stress on the self-actualizing quality of the human organism as the motivating force in therapy," and to develop "a concern with the process of personality change, rather than with the structure of personality." Since Rogers' focus is on a change in the mode of experience by the other person, his approach is practicable with all types of persons, including the so called healthy ones. Hence, it could serve as a basis of sound coaching.

Protreptic could sign up to these principles except for the one

---

37 Kirschenbaum, H. & Henderson Land, V.: Carl Rogers. Dialogues. London. Constable 1990. p.10.

which attempts a personality change. This can never be the target of dialogue, being all too pervading in relation to the other. However, it is of utter importance to protreptic when Rogers states that

> *"I believe it is the presence of certain attitudes in the therapist, which are communicated to, and perceived by, his client, that effect success in psychotherapy. ... These three conditions are the therapist's congruence or genuineness; unconditional positive regard, a complete acceptance; and a sensitively accurate empathetic understanding."*[38]

What the protreptic guide must do besides being able to have an intense feeling for the other person's existence and unique being, is to incorporate the earnestness of reflection, and the unbiased, critical attitude toward concepts and the values covered by them, and a detached, but generous relation to one's self.

As Rogers says, empathy must be active, and this is exactly what the protreptic guide must do, he must effectuate, "parainesis", the admonishing of the other to honor himself through a philosophical attitude, and thus assist him in rebuilding himself. In this sense protreptic is not just urging, but is genuinely edifying. It must, of course, never be reproaching.

However, there is one marked difference between the approach of protreptic on the one side, and Rogers' therapy and most other therapeutic models on the other, namely that the protreptic guide never allows himself to think that he can understand the other. He knows that the other person through his optics must be a construction of the event. In this sense protreptic follows the postmodern legacy in being anti-naturalistic, and hence, pragmatic in the positive sense of the word. What happens between the interlocutors in the dialogue is what counts.

Protreptic shares the unconditional care and kindness towards the other with the attitude of Rogers' therapist, it shares his warnings against external interpretations, but it does not share his

---

38 Ibd 10-11. The dealing with Rogers here is indebted to a master thesis of Tobias dam Hede and Thomas Mosfeldt: "The problem of Symmetry in Coaching – a theoretical Investigation." It was written at the Copenhagen Coaching Centre, 2009.

worries about advice, and suggestions, even if it shares his rejection of any judgment.[39] However, interpretations are the conditions of any dialogue unless we were machines. What must be excluded are not external interpretations as such, but all interpretations which are not reconstructions of the grids of values, and their work. What passes judgment, is not the person, but the values which he embodies, and the way in which he embodies them.

However, what Rogers believes, that genuine empathy is able to contribute with, is also the aim of protreptic:

> *"When he (the client) is thus in contact with his inward experiencing, he can recognize the points at which his experience is at variance with his concept of himself and, consequently, where he is endeavoring to live by a false conception. Such recognition of congruence is the first step towards its resolution and the revision of the concept of self to include the hitherto denied experiences."*[40]

There is an important difference though, because protreptic must be extremely directed towards the historical and social dimension of values. Hence, "congruence" must always be seen as a product of the event of dialogue, as it is produced by the socio-historical settings of events, and thus there can never be an absolute concept of congruence. Proteptic is not liable to commit "the fallacy of the emotional" by thinking that emotions cannot deceive. An emotion is never more than an embodied thought, and hence, intellectualization is the only real means to become master in one's own house. Autonomy is produced by reason. This is the maxim of protreptic, and its Stoic legacy.

A concession is appropriate here. Of course the sense of the event demanded from the protreptic guide must also involve a sense of the other person. Both aspects are products of individual experience, but they do not have the shape of meaning, they exist as significance. The *sense of significance* gives us a forewarning of the other person, a readiness and a platform for dialogue without

---

39 Rogers, ibd. p. 21.
40 Rogers, ibd. p. 16.

which protreptic would be a dogmatically controlled catastrophe. As written earlier we must try to feel the Third I of the other person. Of course different people have different powers of empathy, and the protreptic guide must have developed these capacities to a very high level. So it must be admitted that there is such a thing as a talent of protreptic.

Symmetry is established in the dialogue through the fact that the protreptic guide himself is a victim of socio-economic pressures, ideologies, and of false opinions which means that the liberation aimed at must be produced in common. Of course a therapist can hardly think in this way, but the protreptic guide is no therapist; if anything he is a friend and a co-sufferer driven by compassion for freedom of mind.

What the proteptic guide actually offers the other person is a way of being founded on uncompromising reflection. He must demonstrate this in his process of questioning, incorporating existential earnestness. What he can accomplish is, to alter Dylan Thomas a bit, a journey (or a "travelling") from thought's first fever to its plague. And trying to think to the bottom of one's own being is certainly a plague. It means suffering, and it cannot promise relief, but only hope for it. To honor one-self is to love oneself through reflection. But this love is by nature closer to agape than to eros, however passionate it might be. We must not forget that Plato and Aristotle despised "autophilia", the complacency and self-satisfaction making it into the opposite of "epimeleia heautou".

These considerations imply that protreptic has certain limits in its repertoire. It would normally neither favor dreams nor personal narratives, even if it might use them if the other person insists. Consistent with this, it is careful with the use of metaphors as anything but eye-openers to the origin of the concepts of values.

However protreptic is not hostile to the world conjured up by the senses—quite the opposite. After all, a goal of protreptic is the intensification of attention, and hence, to inspire to new ways of looking at the world and on oneself. Here art could play a part.

21.

Protreptic and the arts

Now we shall look at some issues of the protreptic guidance of the dialogical event in relation to art. A further reason to talk about the "new" protreptic is that the use of art is foreign to the protreptic tradition probably inheriting Plato's comprehension as to the knowledge-creating force of art – even if Aristotle whose influence to Western thought was so great during the Middle Ages and who wrote a "Poietic" did not share Plato's consequential rejection of art, although the latter made a performative contradiction since he practiced it himself in his dialogues. The Renaissance inherits this contradiction by being totally influenced by Plato and by developing art to a degree only known by classical Greek, and even conceiving of science and politics as arts. This is due to the fact that art manifests the principle of translocutionarity, and that art is a special way, in all its dimensions and genres, through which the event is created by the ability to receive it. In the genuine artistic attitude, experience and performance unite into one proto-capacity, the sense of judgement. Here modern protreptic differs from the classical Greek, and probably also Roman, attitude to art as mirroring a lower form of experience, the "techne" and not the "episteme", genuine and true knowledge.

Art is a way of transforming experience into knowledge both by hand, words, and through other media. The attitude of many philosophers after World War II was that art is able to match philosophy in relation to the creation of true knowledge of life, and even that art might be the superior media of embodied thinking; or that philosophy ought to develop procedures of experimenting with experience which could be borrowed from art. Heidegger, Adorno and Deleuze seem to think this way already precented by Schopenhauer much earlier.

In relation to the different genres of art we can create laboratories for the guidance of the event:

In relation to musical performance:

It is possible to enlighten through the experience of musical leadership; to promote the consciousness and development of ourselves through the option to practice musical leadership, and to reinforce the capacity of listening, so important for dealing with people.

This can be done through the setting in which leaders at all levels are given the opportunity to direct musical ensembles through very simple codes. This experience might strengthen their ability to lead experts who know more than themselves. To be forced to act as a novice is an excellent test of one's relation to one self, and to other persons. What we meet here is a rehearsal of the phenomenon of event. This is the concept of the director Peter Hanke, who in 2008 published the book *Performance & lederskab – passionen som drivkraft*. ("Performance & Leadership. Passion as the driving force."). Besides the experience of the communicative event in – so to speak – a naked state, some important event-related capacities are made tangible, among others one's own talent for synchronising, for timing, for dynamic precision, for thematic variation, and for the sensitivity to intonation, to the balance between different voices. These are aspects of an easy readiness to transfer symbolically to other domains of leadership.

But musical performance also contributes to the ability of the "leader on trial" to call forth, and to release, the powers of the group to lead itself in the light of excellence. The intimacy of music with the dimensions of bodily experience opens to a new leadership through other practices of being conscious. When the result of this experience with the musical group, whether a choir or a string quartet, is articulated through the guidance of a skilled counsellor, we might be able to contribute to a new language, a new code, in relation to the broad outlines of leadership; in relation to its way of guiding thematic issues; in relation to its refinement and to its subtleties; in relation to its inner centres of harmonic balance. The special tune of the leader might be revealed as an important aspect of the secret of his style. Because even the most bodily being has to be released from its often and even happy existence beyond the realm of words, through the right wording – however, remembering what Mendelssohn once said, "that music is too precise to be put into words", there are limits to this endeavour. Speech drives out the demon – as Kierkegaard said – if the demon should be driven out, after all. So, words do not necessarily have to kill him.

Art postpones dialogue, making its basis and its credibility more strong, but it never totally abandons it. Thus, the song is a hope with a direction, a voyage into space until the echo brings the sound back; and the solo is a call, if not a prayer, for co-sounding. It is this co-sounding, in the capacity of co-passion, which protreptic must make evident, and not least through art. So a protreptic dialogue could reasonably follow on such a musical session, or in other ways incorporate its experience, because values are released and confronted.

In relation to the visual arts:
The capacity to visualise creates the event of interpretation through a guided sensing. The picture, or the sculpture confronts us with a simultaneity in experiencing, both directing our eyes to an immovable totality, and leading it through patterns of seeing without the linear flow of music and writing. We are given the opportunity to practice omnipotence in the capacity of total survey, the dream of leadership. Recently the development of art as moveable event through the whole range of installations in rooms or in nature – fencing the landscape towards the horizon with strings of plastic simulating the ligaments of a secret organism overflowing its own limits, or painting the picture directly on the bushes of the garden – produces new opportunities to the leader. He will be able to confront living laboratories of the tension between an event as artefact and an event as organism, to step into his own challenges as interiors, and into the future as a space presented as place. These opportunities to run along the lines of the future are in the end a protreptic manoeuvre, since it is all about the criteria and values which we use to mould our future in the patterns of necessity. In Denmark such projects were developed by Kristian Hornsleth and Soeren Dahlgaard, and as a means to critical recognition of social relations and possibilities inside the firm by the painter Kent Hansen and Mille Kalsmose.

In the picture, and in the sculpture, knowledge of forms and colours, of movements, and of the relation between foreground and background, is displayed through the transformation to immediate subjects of experience by receiving this experience we reproduce the inherent knowledge in a new way. The visual arts, especially painting, are able to present the event-horizon as a "ri-poso" or "Still-Leben" with the lines of movements incorporated as patterns – to use a Post-modern phrase which by the way is forming a performative contradiction since it has been repeated almost infinitely many times, we have the opportunity to experience a "repetition with a difference"

By setting up meetings and dialogues between artists and leaders we are able to create events in which the relation between attitudes and creativity is made a reflective subject. Art neither just creates simulations of mini-worlds, nor artefacts of scenes to come; it does not implement, but it develops. It opens the door into a fata morgana, in which the things and processes vaguely discerned for our inner eye are met as answers to the united craving. Art can help protreptic, not by promising shamanism or magic, but by conjuring up a sensual soberness. The mysticism met with here is clear as the day.

What the act of painting could especially contribute to in the protreptic session, is the opportunity of the other person to experience translocutionarity "in the nude". Placing a colored blot on the canvas must not be seen as an act of expressing feelings, or inner states, but as a genuine act of mastered chance, in which the blot expresses what could become of it through the next blot. The painter Anette Holmberg has explored these possibilities. Professor Daved Barry developed this concept in a university setting together with Stefan Meisiek. This pattern of becoming in the process of creating demonstrates both the principles of creativity, and the principles of deep reflection, because the pattern created by chance – which actually might be a mistaken expression for the body as a tacit agent – by the process taking place between the one painting and the canvas, little by little becomes necessary. The starting word in protreptic could be understood as such a blot, in which a necessity of reflection is laid bare formed by the dialogue itself, and being its true content.

The protreptic guide must summon the other person to co-form the dialogue like two painters who together paint a picture.

In relation to the theatre:

The drama was probably the first laboratory of the event. Of course
epic is too, but it does not contribute with a direct, physical setting
of the event. As a spectator of, a participator in, and a developer
of dramatic events and courses, the protreptic guide is able to learn
about the requisites and the staging of the event, and by dissec-
tion initiate the other person into his own dramatic conception
of human relations. The drama is the inner side of protreptic, because it enforces us to do two things: To be serious about our own
consciousness, and to partake through empathy in the fate of the
other person. These two attitudes have a common core: love. This
thin, worn concept testifies to the possibility of a totally other way
to relate to living. When the symphony finally reaches its point of
departure, and when the form in the plastic art yields all that life
which, during other circumstances, would have seeped away in the
experience-machines of time and movement, art accomplishes an
emotion close to the one which should be the subject of "love".
Deliberately contradicting the canonical word-sense one could
state that there is an "eros" for "agape", a passion for love. When
the narrative eternally postpones the end until the phantom-arrival
of the last, truthful reader, then we confront another type of will,
the one whose essence is an attention and a loyalty enriched by
gentleness. One real attitude towards the event is gentleness. This
fact answers to the task of guarding the secret of the event, and at
the same time keeping it forever young by recreating it. Gentleness
is also the capacity of doing protreptic, and when it, at the same
time, is directed towards the other person, and towards ourselves
as a form of self-respect, then its green word-fingers shall make
another knowledge grow, through the intensity and richness of
experience, something which otherwise would have been neglected
and left out. We are then able to act with a mimetic precision, which
can be seen as steps in a count-down, the climax of which is the
freedom earned through the insight into necessity. The true art of
protreptic is to be able to exemplify the possibility of guarding the
balance between freedom and necessity.

Ever since the performances and theories of August Boreal and
the rise of environmental theatre, interactivity in the literal sense
has been an option for drama. "Tamara-land" concepts run for

years in the USA, professor David Boje named his journal after it, and the Danish group "Signa" has recently developed the concept further. The Danish instructor Bent Noergaard, the director of the Centre for Art and Science at the University of South Denmark, and I, developed further his amazing concept of devising entrepreneurial and managerial experiences with creativity as a protreptic setting for organizations.

Theories about these relations were developed by the professors Rob Austin, Daved Barry, Pierre Guillet de Monthoux and Stefan Meisiek.

In relation to the epic:

The epic is the attempt to inscribe the event into a contextual course; its mark is teleology, finality, even if it is only virtually given, rendering the recognition of patterns to the reader. The epic has an energy which comes from its wish to connect events in a way which constitutes a course which satisfies understanding. Epics always try to answer, or even to anticipate, the question, "Why did it happen?", "Why did it happen just like this?" However, the power of good epics is to be able not to sacrifice the equivocal in the very heart of the event explained. Underneath any epic text of quality another event horizon lies, closer to chaos than the ordered patterns of the narrative, but also closer to another order of events. The confrontation with skilled writers, excellent stories, in the media of texts and pictures, could be a lesson of the event, because the event is always inscribed into the context of epic contexts. The logic of epic frames is shaped through four figures of speech:

The "I wanted, was able to, did this thing, because…" The "This happened like this, because…" The "He/she wanted, was able, did like this, because…" And the "We wanted, were able to, did, like this, because…"

The myths inherent in powerful epics were, and are able to put forward claims to territory, to launch the justice of causes, to legitimise the getting hold of allies, and to create the sense of purpose and of community.

Epic does not differ from drama by having one voice only. Often it consists of dialogues too, but it has at least one imaginary voice, a voice behind the voices, which manifests itself more salient than the voice of the playwright, through an omnipresence – in the film this voice is mixed with an anticipated way of seeing, or even with a silent language of tacit gestures, cultivated in the silent movie to a level of mimetic drama far beyond the pantomime. However, this background voice, this hidden way of seeing, these codes of silent gestures, always call for justice by conjuring fate or even providence. In the great text, there is an immense tension between this ordered world of a possible justice and the underlying levels of event horizons incorporating fate, chaos,, power and nonsense. The greater the text, the vaster the shadow of non-sense cast by it.

Protreptic, attempting the realisation of legitimisation in the very core of the inner capillaries of life, has a special relation to epic. It summons the one who has taken permission for telling the truth of our lives. It challenges this authority and this patent. It creates the advent of freedom in the event by revealing the values which direct the course of events. Protreptic seeks the secret level of event horizons hidden in the narrative being without fear of chaos and nonsense. Actually nonsense could be an instrument of revealing the abysses of sense, and the swamps of all the words which have lost their meaning through excessive use and now are forming a putrefying dangerous and deceptive ground for knowledge.

Hence, epic could, in its narrative dimension, be used to unmask the strategies of the narrative itself and penetrate its alluring power by asking who the author really is; and the subject shall always be both the battle of values, and the battle between the nonsense of the reality constructed by common sense and insight.

I myself tried my hand on writing two volumes of philosophical short stories with the task of embodying values and philosophical problems in the narrative without – hopefully – doing wrong to the claims of literature to autonomy.

In relation to poetry:

When Plato was tired of poets he used to say that a poem should be written out in discursive language in order to see what it could carry of rational sense. This is, of course, unfair towards poetry, even if a lot of poets might deserve this criticism, and it is quite appropriate in relation to bad examples of allegorical and mannerist art. However, it might be the core of how protreptic could make use of poetry, since many people are fascinated with the secret significance lying in-between or perhaps even "behind" lyric phrases. The challenge to interpret could be an alternative to begin the protreptic dialogue, or to guide it on if it has come to a deadlock, because an interpretation always has some criteria, and any criteria is based on values. Also the opportunity to express himself lyrically would give the other person the chance to articulate significance, and hence, the way in which he lives his values.

The mode of a poem is important, and the discursive phrasing of this could point to the order of mental universe of the other person. The chance to express the mood of a poem might be a particularly viable alternative entrance to a dialogue.

In relation to dance:

Dance is the essence of performance. It mimes participation. Dancers in residence could act out a carnival, be dancing congresses, kind competitors, and brave consultants, dancing hand in hand. A ballet, a pavane, a chaconne, a gigue, or a reel shall transform reality into a moveable feast. The concept of the ritual, with its air of buzz words, can appear from the depths of organisational reason, dressed in the vestiges of an old, both Apollonian and Dionysian, cosmogony, challenging the terrible threat of the organisation: banality, boredom, and triviality. Dance is able to re-enchant through a transparent massiveness in bodies acting, moving, drawing bonds, and losing them again, invoking chthonic laughter, and Olympic humour. Because we always want spirits to enforce and art to enchant, if our ending should not be despair.

Professor Lis Engel at the University of Copenhagen has recently dug into such liberating possibilities of dance.

Protreptic has the power to deny the temptation of both the "amor fati", and the escapism of the phantasm. By its practice it conjures up an infinite bond of dancing human beings hand in hand, because like joy, the state of mind which it inflicts is contagious. "We must know commonwealth again from bitter searching of the heart, we must rise to play a greater part".

22.

The leader as a protreptic guide

There are serious problems connected with the leader functioning as a protreptic guide. This does not mean that protreptic does not belong in the organization—it could be a proper goldmine for HR—but many ethical and contextual problems arise when this method is adapted to managerial purposes; some problems of which are similar to those of the coaching manager and some of which are different.

I. Protreptic both presupposes that a transformation from manager to leader has taken place, and that it reinforces and produces this change. Protreptic is not a proper strategic instrument, but it might do wonders for an organisation.

II. Protreptic is not another form of coaching, because it refuses any agendas except to liberate the other person, and because it seeks total symmetry. Thus it cannot be built on an authority of power, knowledge, or information – even if the protreptic guide seems invested with at least a power of knowledge of the protreptic event. The other person must be seen as a human being only, not as an employee; and so must the leader. This demands a firm ethical attitude of the leader, because he must not expect to be heard or answered as a leader. However, this demands much of the employee too, because he is the one who must expose himself.

III. This demands a very high level of attentiveness by the leader; the slightest tendency towards confession on behalf of the other person must be stopped immediately by him, and so must any attempt from his side of being mate-like. Joviality, over-friendliness, and deliberate intimacy, must be avoided. The protreptic guide must be extremely aware of the event of dialogue, and he must be able to handle any undertone of servility, resentment, or feeling injured by the employee. The task of liberating the dialogical event from its institutional power-setting is a Sisyphean labour.

IV. The result of such a protreptic dialogue might be either a confrontation of values, or a realization by the worker of the fact that his real interests are not met by the organisation. It is also not unlikely that the leader himself might feel the same way, and that he then is caught in a dilemma, or, that he would realize that the organization does not meet his desires either. So the protreptic dialogue guided by a leader might not always be a win-win situation for the company, but may still possibly be for the interlocutors after all. Such crises of loyalty are unpleasant, especially when the leader produces them himself. The opportunity to come into contact with one's mental world, and the patterns of self, might have an explosive effect. On the other hand, new insights and loyalties could be produced, which could never be reached in another way.

V. As a means of enriching the schemes of appraisal interviews (the yearly interviews of employees guided by the responsible manager), the schemes of registering psychical work-environment (in Denmark private and public organisations must make periodical evaluations not only of the physical work-environment but also of the psychic), and work-climate generally, protreptic is unsurpassed. Also before a 360 degree investigation of managers it would enrich the production of answers and the mutual understanding of them to have a protreptic dialogue in plenum. Recently the Confederation of Danish Industry has taken up protreptic in this context.

There are many models of how employees can be involved in protreptic dialogues and conversations.

The classical one is where the protreptic guide is alone with the other person, and the guide is somebody who is in possession of a certain level of "phronesis". He could be a philosopher, but also any other person, who is not involved with the other person through shared working relations or other economic or institutional connections. The only criterion of being able to function as a protreptic guide is to possess "phronesis". If the leader has this capacity many of the barriers for his ability to evade the problems of symmetry and ethics produced by the organisational setting would disappear.

The protreptic guide who possesses "phronesis" masters a reflective thought which can grasp totality. It is able to survey the event. The principle of virtue ("areté") is embodied in "phronesis". Let me repeat some of that which was already said about "phronesis" in chapter 18 in order to make the demands on the leader in this role explicit.

Often "phronesis" will be translated with "wisdom", but of the two Latin translations of the word, "prudentia" and "sapientia", it must certainly be the latter, even if it does not fit the Greek sense properly, because it is a mode of experiencing the other person directed by values, by the normative perspective.

Recent managerial literature has criticized the broad tendency to identify phronesis with prudency, thus suppressing the all important normative dimension.[41]

"Phronesis" is the precondition of all ethical and moral action, and it is both an autonomous capacity, which unites knowledge and force of action, and a capacity incorporated in the insight into and practice of every virtue. In this capacity "phronesis" is a "tropos", a basic attitude which expresses the will and the ability to do the good for the good's own sake, and the will and ability to practice the other three Greek cardinal virtues (phronesis is the fourth one), courage ("andreia"), self-command ("sophrosyne"), and justice ("dikaiósyne"). That is why Plato could state that he who masters one virtue must master them all, because they presuppose "phronesis" and thus automatically imply a general normative attitude.

The creation and development of "phronesis" is clearly the goal of protreptic. "Phronesis" is the capacity to be alive for the event, but this attitude is a normatively guided sense, not just "practical wisdom". "Phronesis" then must designate the principle of self-reflection in the event, when it is directed towards the development and honoring of the self. "To phronema" means the specific sense of self, the opening towards the "Third I". Conceived in this way "phronesis" is incorporated in a process of normative self-creation, which is called a "hexis", a deliberate spiral-movement of an increased capacity of ethical earnestness and imagination. Thus is it

---

41 Stattler, M & Roos, J. (2006): 'Reframing strategic preparedness: an essay on practical wisdom'. *Int. J. Management Concepts and Philosophy*, Vol. 2, No. 2, pp. 99–117. And Stattler, M., Roos, J., Victor B.: Illustrating the need for Practical Wisdom. *Management Concepts and Philosophy,* Vol. 2, No. 1, 2006. *And* Stattler, M., Roos, J. Victor, B. (2007): "Dear Prudence: An Essay on Practical Wisdom in Strategy Making". *Social Epistemology*, Volume 21, Issue 2 April 2007

treated by Aristotle in his *Nicomachean Ethic,* referring to an inner force. "Phronesis" is not based on certain knowledge, because it deals with the "endechomenon", with that which could be otherwise. True knowledge, "episteme", deals with that, which can be proved, and of which we know the necessary and sufficient conditions of its existence, but that which could be otherwise cannot be proven, it must be the subject of intuition ("nous"). "Phronesis" is thinking and action guided by values, and based on deliberation, and choice, or decision, "proairesis", relating to that which is good or bad for a human being, but which cannot be subject of certainty. In opposition to "episteme", "phronesis" is not only theoretical knowledge, but deals with the concrete and is in a way related to induction, to an experience-based increase in knowledge about the good by doing it. Thus "phronesis" is the epistemological concept of self-forming, "hexis", guided by the maxim "epimeleia heautou", "to take care of oneself". From these deliberations we have deduced that *a value is a "phronetic" capacity.*

Phronesis is also the sense of the event and the sense of the possible.

The "phronetic" aspect presents itself as an event-bound evaluation of the right to do: it is an act of placing an emphasis. Through this process the self is posited. In the moment of the event the values involved and realized create identity. It is an act among possible attitudes in which the decision itself constitutes the necessity of the course of actions. A value makes an attitude necessary through retroactive validity.

The consequence of this determination of the concept of value is that it is legitimated through the sense of significance. The value shows us the power of the "Third I", and its reality, because the reflective dialogue between I-1 and I-2 producing the decision of this value fetches its direction and its validity from the presence of the "Third I" as a resonance.

Any person who has worked thoroughly on the normative creation of himself will have passed through modes of protreptic dialogues with himself. Our culture is not a proteptic one, because we seem to prefer psychological and not axiological images of identity, but every person should be able to take part in protreptic, at least as one who is guided.

We must abstract ourselves from the teacher-pupil relationship and look at every person as having the full capacity to accomplish a protreptic dialogue with himself, if he really wants. The protreptic guide is the incubator of this process, its facilitator, but not a teacher. He just demonstrates the obviousness of seeking freedom by being the master in one's own house.

This opens a wide space of possibilities for protreptic. The obstacles are power-relations and unwillingness to reflect.

So, if the leader should function as a protreptic guide he must be in possession of the capacity of "phronesis".

Since this capacity cannot become part of an instrumental relation with other people, it is not a means of managerial strategy. However, strategy could in a wider sense consist in assisting people to be masters in their own lives by knowing their own basic values, and acting on behalf of them. But the leader cannot pursue this goal unless the whole organization is structured in this direction.

The private enterprise is not normally seen as a place of converting people to the ethically good, but a language of a governmental type using terms imported from political philosophy like "corporate citizen", and the deafening talk about personal development, suggest a more morally concerned attitude towards the organizational world and the employed individual. In the public sector, where such attitudes should be expected, almost the opposite development can be traced in municipalities that do not have leaders who are able to take a stand against political ideologies of effectiveness. It is even at work in the Danish ministries. Here the employees meet working conditions, which only a few would put up with in the private sector.

Since intimate technologies are increasing in all organizations, the capacity to make values real and to lead proper dialogues becomes more and more urgent. Protreptic is unmatched as a procedure here. So leaders simply *must* learn to do protreptic and to further protreptic conversations at all levels, horizontally and vertically. Protreptic conversations can be performed by employees at all levels in groups of up to 10-12 people. They can be performed by leaders and employees together, by local line leaders, chiefs of departments, by CEO's, and so on, and by low level employees alone, or together with one or more leaders. Whether these conversations need a protreptic guide, a person with some knowledge of this method, or just someone from the group playing the role, must be determined by the situation.

The crucial point is that any organization must work on an educational program in protreptic, because protreptic is the one and only basis for the creation of a new organizational culture in which people relate with care to others and to themselves. The alternative is conceiving work as non-identity-forming or as a place of pain and fatigue (the original sense of the word "labor" though), and to ignore the increasing problems of life-work-balance, attitudes which I do not believe in.

This is the reason why I wrote this book.

Litterature

Aristotle (1926): *On Sophistical Refutations. On Coming-to-be and Passing Away. On the Cosmos.* (Loeb) Cambridge Mass.: Cambridge University Press.

Aristotle (1936): *On the Soul. Parva Naturalia. On Breath.* (Loeb) Cambridge Mass.: Cambridge University Press.

Aristotle (1960): *Posterior analytics and Topica.* Loeb. Cambridge Mass.: Harvard University Press.

Aristotle (2005): *Protreptikos. Hinführung zur Philosophie* (Greek/German). Rekonstruiert, übersetzt und kommentiert von Gerhart Schneeweiss. Darmstadt: Wisenschaftliche Buchgesellschaft.

Aristotle (1994): *The Nicomachean Ethics.* Loeb. Harvard University Press.

Aristotle (1994): *The Art of Rhetoric.* Loeb. Harvard University Press.

Aristotle (1995): *De anima.* Loeb. Harvard University Press.

Aristotle (1995): *Poetics.* Loeb. Harvard University Press.

Aristotle (1960): Posterior analytics and Topica. Loeb. Cambridge Mass.: Harvard University Press.

Aristotle (1926): On Sophistical Refutations. On Coming-to-be and Passing Away. On the Cosmos. (Loeb)Cambridge Mass.: Cambridge University Press.

Aristotle (1936): On the Soul. Parva Naturalia. On Breath (Loeb). Cambridge Mass.: Cambridge University Press.

Badiou A. (2006): *Being and Event.* New York: Continuum.

Bergson, H. (2007/1912): Matter and Memory. New York: Cosimo Classics.

Barthes R. (2006): *Empire of Signs.* Hill and Wang.

Blaug, R. (2000): 'Citizenship and political judgment: between discourse ethics and phronesis', *Res Publica*, Vol. 6, pp. 179-198.

Czarniawska, B. (1997): *Narrating the organization: Dramas of institutional identity.* Chicago, IL: University of Chicago Press.

Czarniawska, B. (1998): *A narrative approach to organization studies.* Thousand Oaks, CA: Sage.

Clegg, S. and Ross-Smith, A. (2003): 'Revisiting the boundaries: management education and learning in a post-positivist world', *Academy of Management Learning and Education*, Vol. 2,

Deleuze, G. (1990): *The Logic of Sense*. New York: Columbia University Press.

Deleuze, G. (1994): *Difference and Repetition*. New York: Columbia University press.

Deleuze, G. & Guattari, F.: (1994): *What is Philosophy*. London, New York: Verso.

Diogenes Laertius (1995): *Lives of Eminent Philosophers*. Loeb. Harvard University Press.

Eikeland, O. (2001) 'Action research as the hidden curriculum of the western tradition', in P. Reason and H. Bradbury (Eds.) *Handbook of Action Research: Participative Inquiry and Practice*, London: Sage.

Eikeland, O. (2008): *The Ways of Aristotle. Aristotelian phrónêsis, Aristotelian Philosophy of Dialogue, and Action Research*. Bern: Peter Lang.

Epictetus (1996): *Encheiridion*. Loeb. Harvard University Press.

Guillet de Monthoux, P. (2004): *The Art Firm: Aesthetic Management and Metaphysical Marketing*, Stanford University Press, Palo Alto.

Gadamer, H.-G. (2002): *Truth and Method*, New York: Continuum.

Gray, J. (2004): *Consciousness: Creeping up on the Hard Problem*. Oxford: Oxford University Press.

Heidegger, M.(1967): *Sein und Zeit*. Tübingen: Max Niemeyer Verlag.

Hegel, G.W.F. (1967: *Enzyklopädie der philosophischen Wissenshaften*. Berlin: Hegel-Instiut: 2007.

Jaeger, W. (1989): *Paideai. Die Formung des griechischen Menschen*. Berlin/ New York: Walter de Gruyter.

Kearney, R (2002): *On Stories*. New York: Routledge.

Kirkeby, O.F. (1994) *Event and Body-Mind. An Analytical-Hermeneutic Investigation*. (Danish) Aarhus: Modtryk.

Kirkeby, O.F.(2005): *Eventum tantum– the Ethos of the Event*. (Danish) København: Samfundslitteratur.

Kirkeby, O.F (2006): *The Event of Beauty– the Aesthetics of the Event*. (Danish) København: Samfundslitteratur.

Kirkeby, O.F. (2007): *Management of the Event and the Force of Action*. (Danish) København: Samfundslitteratur.

Kirkeby, O.F. (2008): *The Virtue of Leadership*. Copenhagen Business School Press.

Kirkeby, O.F. (2003): "The Greek Square, or, the Normative Challenge of Aesthetics". *Ephemera* 2003; vol. 3, nr. 3, s. 197-219

Kirkeby, O.F. (2004): "Eventum Tantum: To Make the World Worthy of What Could Happen To It." *Ephemera* vol 4(3) 2004

Kirkeby, O.F. (2008): *The Self Happens – the Event of Consciousness.* København: Samfundslitteratur.

Kirkeby, O.F. (2009): *The New Protreptic. The concept and the Art.* Copenhagen Business School Press (forthcoming).

Libet, B. (1985): "Unconscious cerebral initiative and the role of conscious will in voluntary action". *Behavioral and Brain Sciences*, 8: 529-566.

Lipsius, J. (1998): *De constantia. Von der Standhaftigkeit*, ed. Florian Neumann, Excerpta Classica, 16 Mainz: Dieterich'sche Verlagsbuchhandlung.

Macintyre, A. (1984) *After Virtue*, South Bend, IN: University of Notre Dame Press.

Merleau-Ponty, M. (1962): *Phenomenology of Perception*, Routledge, London.

Mintzberg, H. and Waters, J. (1985) 'Of strategies, deliberate and emergent', *Strategic Management Journal*, Vol. 6, pp. 257-272.

Cusanus, N. (): *De li non aliud*. Hamburg: Felix Meiner 1979.

Plato (1995): *Phaedrus*. Loeb. Harvard University Press.

Plato (2000): *The Republic*. Harvard University Press.

Plato (2001): *Philebus*. Loeb. Harvard University Press.

Plato (2001): *Laws (Nomoi)*. Loeb. Harvard University Press.

Plato (2001): *Symposium*. Loeb. Harvard University Press.

Plato (2001): *Meno & Protagoras*. Loeb. Harvard University Press.

Polenz, M. (1992): *Die Stoa. Geschichte einer geistigen Bewegung.* 7. edt. Göttingen: Vandenhoeck & Ruprecht.

P. Ricoeur (1984): *Time and Narrative*. Chicago: University of Chicago Press.

Sletteroed, N.A. (2009): *Det skapende menneske. Anthropos ergazesthai. Uttlegning av Genesins ontology & parousias ontology. En begivenhedsfilosofisk ansats til "Det Godes" nærværs-protreptik* (Creative man. Anthropos ergazesthai. An interpretation of the ontology of genesein & the ontology of parousia. An event-philosophical attempt to "The presence-protreptic" of "The Good"). (The thesis is in Norwegian).

Stattler, M & Roos, J. (2006): 'Reframing strategic preparedness: an essay on practical wisdom'. *Int. J. Management Concepts and Philosophy*, Vol. 2, No. 2, pp. 99-117.

Stattler, M., Roos, J., Victor B.: Illustrating the need for Practical Wisdom. *Management Concepts and Philosophy,* Vol. 2, No. 1, 2006.

Stattler, M. & Roos, J. (2007): "Dear Prudence: An Essay on Practical Wisdom in Strategy Making". *Social Epistemology*, Volume 21, Issue 2 April 2007, pp. 151 – 167.

Sternberg, R. (1998): 'A balance theory of wisdom', *Review of General Psychology*, Vol. 2, No. 4, pp. 347-365.

Tsoukas, H. and Cummings, S. (1997): 'Marginalization and recovery: the emergence of Aristotelian themes in organization studies', *Organization Studies*, Vol. 18, No. 4, pp. 655-683.

Whitehead, A.N. (1985): *Process and Reality*. New York: The Free Press.